HIDDEN TRUTHS

HIDDEN TRUTHS

Young people's experiences of running away

Gwyther Rees
Leeds Safe House

The Children's Society

MAKING LIVES WORTH LIVING

A Voluntary Society Of The Church Of England And The Church In Wales

Charity Registration No.221124

First published in 1993 by
The Children's Society
Edward Rudolf House
Margery Street
London WC1X 0JL

A catalogue record of this book is available from the British Library.

ISBN 0 907324 82 7

Typeset and printed by
The Grange Press
Butts Road, Southwick, Sussex

Contents

Acknowledgements

The completion of this research was heavily dependent on the willingness of young people to contribute their experiences and views. Thanks are therefore due to all the young people who took part in the research by completing questionnaires or by participating in interviews.

The research was also only possible because of the cooperation and assistance of local agencies. Arthur Giles and Alison Hodgson of Leeds City Council Educational Welfare Service provided considerable assistance during the planning of the research. Young people and workers at "Y" Training Services were helpful during the piloting of the school survey questionnaire. Staff in the following agencies and departments contributed to the research either by taking part in interviews or by assisting with the administration of the surveys:

> Leeds City Council Education Department (educational welfare officers, youth workers and teachers)
> Leeds City Council Social Services Department (senior managers, social workers, and residential care staff)
> West Yorkshire Probation Service
> Hawksworth YMCA
> Middleton YWCA
> West Yorkshire Police

Finally, on a personal level, I would like to thank the research consultant to the project and colleagues at Leeds Safe House for their support and encouragement throughout the three years of this research.

Research Consultant:
Mike Stein
Child Care Research and Development Unit, Department of Adult Continuing Education, University of Leeds.

INTRODUCTION

"People like me run away for reasons. I mean what's the point if you've got a nice warm home, and you've got no problems at all - you've got no need to run away. It's not very enjoyable, it's not a laughing matter, it's not glamorous or anything. But if you have got problems or things are going wrong and you can't cope, then you run away like I did."
(Young person interviewed as part of the research)

This report is concerned with the issue of young people under 16 who run away or are forced to leave their homes. The phenomenon of young people running away is not a new one. There is historical evidence of street children in London as far back as the 1850s (Frost and Stein, 1989). However, it is only in the last ten years or so that the issue has received much attention in the UK.

Research carried out by The Children's Society using nation-wide missing person statistics for 1986 and 1987 indicated that there were at least 98,000 reported incidents involving missing young people during that year (Newman, 1989). This research also included a study of 532 young people who had used the country's first refuge for young people. More recently a research study by National Children's Home, again using missing person statistics, supported Newman's estimates and went some way towards challenging popular conceptions about running away, in particular the idea that young people run away to the bright lights (Abrahams and Mungall, 1992).

Valuable as these studies have been, they only cover incidents of running away which have been reported by adults and have been officially recorded. It is clear then that they cannot estimate the incidence of running away which goes unreported. Moreover, they provide very little reliable information about the reasons why young people run away from home and what happens to them while they are away. Therefore, there are still large gaps in our knowledge and understanding of the issue of young people running away.

The research findings presented in this report go some way towards filling this information gap. The research in this report was carried out as part of The Children's Society's Leeds Safe House

1

project, currently one of the few projects in England offering refuge to young people under 16 who run away or are forced to leave where they live.

Research aims

The aims of the research were:
1. To estimate the number and characteristics of young people who run away in Leeds
2. To highlight the experiences of these young people.
In fulfilling these aims it was hoped that the research would contribute to a greater understanding of running away and the related issues that affect young people.

Research methods

The research was carried out using the following methods:
1. A survey of young people
A survey of 1,234 young people in 12 secondary schools in Leeds was carried out. As far as we know this is the first survey of its kind in the country, gathering first hand information from a large, representative sample of young people aged 14 to 16 by means of a questionnaire. A small supplementary survey (35 young people) was carried out in nine children's homes in Leeds in order to reach a larger number of young people living in residential care. A similar supplementary survey was attempted for young people regularly absent from school. Unfortunately the response rate for this survey was too low for the results to be valid. Finally, questionnaires were also completed by 80 young people staying at Leeds Safe House (a refuge for young people, usually under 16, who run away or are forced to leave where they live).
2. In-depth interviews with young people
Interviews were carried out with 28 young people with recent experience of running away. Most of the interviews were tape recorded and transcribed word for word, and therefore provide rare descriptive data relating to the issue of running away in young people's own words.
3. Interviews with professionals
During the early stages of the research, interviews were conducted with a range of 30 professionals (including social services staff,

teachers, educational welfare officers, probation officers, youth workers and police officers) who work with young people in three contrasting areas of Leeds.

The research therefore provides detailed information, in both statistical and descriptive form, about young people's experiences of running away. All the information (with the obvious exception of the interviews with professionals) was collected directly from young people.

Layout of the report

A summary of the key findings of the research follows this introduction. The main body of the report begins by presenting findings on the numbers of young people running away in Leeds, based on the schools survey, and compares these findings with previous research (Chapter 1). The remainder of findings of the schools survey are then presented, covering the characteristics of young people who run away, and their experiences while they are away from home (Chapters 2 to 4). Quotes from the in-depth interviews with young people have been incorporated into these chapters to illustrate key points. Chapter 5 deals with the issue of young people running away from residential care, making use of both the residential care and schools surveys. The remaining two chapters concentrate on the findings of the in-depth interviews with young people. First, the complex issue of why young people run away from where they live is examined (Chapter 6). Second, young people's experiences of adults' responses to their running away are discussed (Chapter 7). Information from the interviews with professionals and from the questionnaires completed at Leeds Safe House has been used at various points throughout the report to supplement the other material. The conclusion draws together the main findings of the research, discusses the policy and practice implications of the findings, and highlights specific areas where further research seems to be particularly needed.

Whilst the research concentrated on one particular city, the experiences of young people in Leeds will be similar to those of young people in any other large city in the UK. The findings presented in this report should be of interest to anyone concerned with the issue of running away, or the welfare of young people in general.

Summary of key findings

All the statistical findings presented in this summary are estimates based on the surveys carried out in schools and residential care. The statistical significance of the findings are discussed, where appropriate, in the main body of the report and further information is provided in the Appendix.

● One in seven young people in Leeds runs away from home, and stays away overnight, before the age of 16 [page 9].

● There are over 2,400 incidents of running away from home overnight each year in Leeds, which is an average of six or seven incidents per day [page 9].

● Over 1000 young people in Leeds run away from home overnight for the first time each year [page 9].

● Young people run away for a wide variety of reasons. For the young people who took part in research interviews some of the main underlying reasons for running away were:
> Physical violence
> Emotional abuse and neglect
> Sexual abuse
> Power struggles with parents/carers
> Negative experiences of being taken into care and
> of the care "system"
> Bullying in care
> Peer pressure

One of the main motivations for young people to run away often seems to be to escape these situations, but there is also evidence of young people being forced to leave home by their parents at ages as young as 13 [pages 44 to 63].

● Females are more likely to run away from home than males - 17% compared to 11% [page 10].

- There are large differences in running away rates among young people of different ethnic origins [page 15].

- There is a link between running away and truancy [page 18].

- Young people who have lived in residential care are more likely to have run away than young people who have never lived in care. However, the findings also suggest that most young people who run from residential care had run away from their family before they ever went into care [page 39].

- Most young people who run away do so only once or twice [page 20].

- One in nine young runaways had started running away before the age of 11 [page 21].

- Many young people (42%) had slept rough the last they time they ran away [page 24].

- Very few people who ran away approached professional agencies for help or advice while they were away from home [page 25].

- Friends are the main source of support for young people while they are away from home [page 25].

- Most young runaways return home of their own accord. In many cases the situation that caused them to run away is not resolved, and they may be punished for having run away. In addition, young people who repeatedly run away often feel that adults involved with them have not listened to the reasons why they ran away, or paid attention to their needs [page 31].

CHAPTER ONE

How many young people run away?

"I've noticed on the streets that there's more young people running away than there have been - and people are getting younger. Perhaps now young people realize when things are wrong. When I was young I didn't realize that some of the things that happened to me were wrong. But when I saw Childline on TV I realized they were wrong"
(Young person, aged 18, who has been running away regularly over a 10 year period)

One of the main aims of the survey was to estimate the number of young people running away in Leeds. This was an important aim: running away is only beginning to be recognized as an important issue in Britain and, despite increased media attention, there is still a tendency to deny the extent of the problem. For example, one head teacher responded to our request to carry out the survey by stating:

"At this school we do not have a problem of children running away from home. I do not think that there would be any useful purpose served in this school participating in the survey."

Following this letter a nearby school serving the same geographical area was selected as an alternative and it was found that 30% of the young people had run away.

Previous research

It was recognized from the outset of the research that there is no clear definition of the term 'running away'. The small amount of previous research in Britain (Newman, 1989; Abrahams and Mungall, 1992) has made use of police statistics on reported missing persons to reach an estimate of the number of young people running away. On this basis Newman estimated that there were 98,000

6

reported incidents of missing young people in England, Scotland, Northern Ireland and Wales each year. Abrahams and Mungall estimated that 43,000 young people under 18 run away every year in England and Scotland, accounting for 102,000 running away incidents. They also estimate that, in the four areas they surveyed, between two and six young people per 1,000 run away from home each year.

These two pieces of research have made an important contribution to knowledge about missing young people. However, their figures are likely to be underestimates because they do not include running away incidents which are not reported to the police. In fact Newman found that only around half of the young people using a refuge in London had been recorded by the police as reported missing. She suggested that one of the reasons for this was poor police recording systems.

Current research

Professionals interviewed in Leeds as part of the current research were consistently of the opinion that many incidents of young people running away from their families go unreported. They put forward several reasons for this:

- In cases where the young person has been mistreated or abused, parent(s) have a vested interest in not involving police or social services.
- The parent(s) may already feel hostility or mistrust towards the police, and as a result be reluctant to involve them.
- The parent(s) may know where the young person is and therefore see no point in reporting the incident.
- The parent(s) may have become used to the young person running away and not bother to report the incident.

It is doubtful, then, whether missing persons statistics accurately describe the incidence of young people running away from home. There is, however, a very high level of reporting of young people running away from residential care as staff have a duty to do this, even in cases where the young person has only been gone a few hours. One further consequence of this is that previous research is likely to have overestimated the proportion of young runaways who are running from residential care (see Chapter 5).

The schools survey

The schools survey approached the issue in an entirely different manner to the previously mentioned research. The data was gathered directly from young people and, following similar research in the US (eg Brennan *et al.*, 1978), the questionnaire allowed young people to define their own situation, rather than trying to impose a rigid definition of running away. This reflects a theme, which comes up throughout this report, that it is only by listening to young people that we can fully understand the issue of running away.

Young people in schools were asked four general questions about running away:

1. Have any of your friends ever run away ?
2. Have you ever run away *during the day* ?
3. Have you ever run away *and stayed away overnight*?
4. Have you ever wanted to run away ?

The results of questions 2 and 3 are shown in Figure 1.

Figure 1
Percentage of young people who had run away

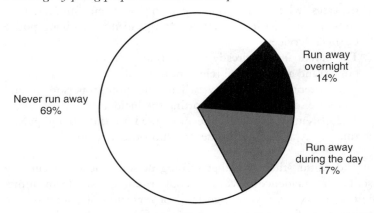

Altogether, nearly a third of the young people surveyed had run away, and almost half of these young people had stayed away

overnight when they had run away. These are surprisingly high figures, and indicate that running away is a common experience
amongst young people, rather than something which only affects a
small minority. Further evidence of this is that over half of the
young people surveyed (54%) had a friend who had run away, and
that almost half of those who had never run away (47%) said that
they had wanted to. It is estimated from the survey results that:

- 14% of young people in Leeds run away from home
  overnight before the age of 16.
- Over 1000 young people in Leeds run away from home
  overnight *for the first time* each year.
- There are over 2,400 incidents of running away from home
  overnight each year in Leeds, which is an average of six or
  seven incidents per day.

The margins of error for the 14% figure are plus or minus 1.8% at
the 95% confidence level. An explanation of how these estimates
were reached is included in the Appendix.

Estimates from the schools survey indicate that 12 young people
per 1,000 in the 5 to 15 year old age group run away from home for
the first time each year. This is considerably higher than Abrahams
and Mungall's estimates of between two and six runaways (not just
first time runaways) per 1,000 in the geographical areas they
covered.

CHAPTER TWO

Which young people run away?

"When I was five I told my teacher what was going on at home, but she told me to stop lying. My mum's very middle class, and a lot of other people in the [child sex] ring were middle class, so all the abuse was really hush-hush. The first time I ran away was when I was eight. I slept in a park for four days."

The design of the survey enables a comparison of running away rates according to gender, family economic background, family constitution, ethnic origin, geographical area and school attendance. This chapter deals with each of these characteristics in turn.

Gender

A key finding of the survey was a significant difference in the running away rates for females and males. 17% of the females surveyed had run away overnight, compared to 11% of the males (see Figure 2). Interestingly, though, a higher percentage of males ran away during the day.

Figure 2. Percentage of females and males running away

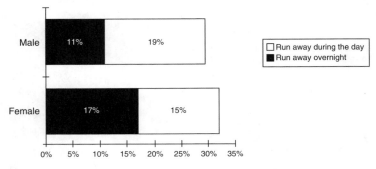

Excluding the small number of young people in the survey who had been in care, it is estimated that 61% of young people who run away from home overnight are females. This estimate is backed up by the experience of the Children's Society's refuge in Leeds - 61% of young people running from home who were referred to the refuge in 1992 were female. A comparison of the patterns of running away for males and females in the survey is to be found in Chapter 4.

Family economic background

Two indicators of family economic background were included in the questionnaire: type of housing, and the number of people in the household with a paid job. Both of these indicators of family economic background need to be viewed with a degree of caution. With the growth in the proportion of people who own their homes and the more recent increase in mortgage debt, property ownership is not as helpful an indicator of affluence as it may have been in the past. Counting the number of people in a household with a paid job does not adequately take into account the large numbers of people who work part-time and have low incomes. The findings in this section must therefore be seen as only tentative indications.

Looking first at type of housing, 73% of the young people's families lived in owner occupied housing, 25% in properties rented off the council, 1% in other rented properties, and 2% in other kinds of accommodation (including young people in residential care). The rates of running away for the young people living in the two main categories of housing were:

Figure 3
Percentage of young people running away by type of family housing

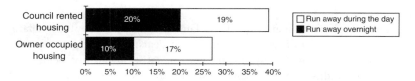

Council rented housing	20%	19%
Owner occupied housing	10%	17%

☐ Run away during the day
■ Run away overnight

0% 5% 10% 15% 20% 25% 30% 35% 40%

   The rate of running away overnight for young people living in council rented accommodation was twice as high as that for young people whose families owned their housing. Statistically there is clear evidence here of a link between type of housing and the incidence of running away.

   As regards family employment situation, only 7% of all young people surveyed lived in families where no one had a paid job. The rate of running away according to family employment situation is shown in the following chart.

Figure 4
Percentage of young people running away by family employment situation

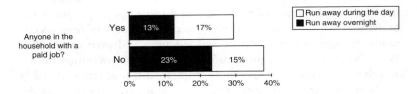

   Again there is a relationship between the family's economic situation (this time in terms of employment) and the incidence of running away from home, with young people from families in which no one has a paid job being more likely to have run away than other young people.

   Despite the drawbacks in the indicators used, the survey does therefore provide some evidence of a link between economic disadvantage (measured in terms of housing and employment) and running away. At the same time, it also illustrates that children from better off families do run away, so running away cannot be explained solely in economic terms.

Family constitution

The effect of the make-up of the family on young people's welfare has been a hotly debated issue in recent years, but previous research on running away (using missing person statistics) has not been able to explore this area. The schools survey therefore represents the first opportunity to explore this issue. Young people were asked to indicate who they lived with, and their answers have been translated into four main family types, according to the adults living in the household: lone parent, both parents, parent and step-parent, and 'other'.

The running away rates for the first three family types are as shown in Figure 5 (the 'Other' category only accounted for 17 young people and it would be misleading to include it in the chart).

Figure 5. Percentage of young people running away by family type

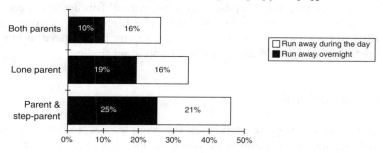

The differences in the rates of running away are large and statistically significant. However, caution is needed in interpreting these results. As has already been shown there is evidence of a link between economic status and running away. Economic factors may be relevant here given that, for example, lone parent families are often economically disadvantaged. Looking only at families living in council rented housing, for example, a different picture emerges:

Figure 6
Percentage of running away by family type for households living in council rented housing[1]

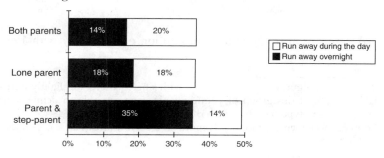

The differences between young people living with both parents and those living with lone parents are now minimal. In fact statistical analysis of the above figures indicates that there is insufficient evidence of a significant difference between the rates of running away of the three family types. A detailed analysis of the inter-relationships between family type, housing type, and running away rates indicated that the direct effect of family type on running away rates is weak, while the effect of housing type (a potential indicator of economic differences) is strong. This is due to the small difference between 'Both parent' families and 'Lone parent' families when economic factors are taken into account. The higher rate of running away in families with a step-parent is even more pronounced in Figure 6 than in Figure 5 and remains an important finding.

Ethnic origin

One consideration in designing the sample was to attempt to include significant numbers of young people from the main ethnic minority groups in Leeds.

Table 1
Ethnic origin of young people in the survey sample

	Number of young people in survey sample	Percentage of survey sample	Percentage of population of Leeds aged 10 to 15 years old[2]
African/Caribbean	40	3.2%	1.1%
Black-other	0		0.9%
Chinese	6	0.5%	0.3%
Indian/Pakistani/Bangladeshi	81	6.6%	6.1%
Mixed origin	15	1.2%	n.a.
White	1071	86.8%	90.2%
Other	11	0.9%	1.4%
Unknown	10	0.8%	n.a.

A comparison of the ethnic constitution of the survey with 1991

---

[1]The housing figures for young people with single parents are slightly unreliable as 12% of this group of young people were not able to define their family housing type (compared to 3% for other young people)
[2]Source: 1991 Census, County Report: West Yorkshire (Part 1), London: HMSO

Census figures indicates that the sampling method was successful in including fairly representative proportions of different ethnic groups, with young people from African/Caribbean and Indian/Pakistani /Bangladeshi backgrounds being slightly over-represented in the survey (see Table 1).

Due to the small numbers in some of the categories, analysis of running away rates can only be carried out for three groups in the survey - African/Caribbean, Indian/Pakistani/Bangladeshi, and White - and even here the results should be treated with caution. The running away rates for the three groups are shown below:

Figure 7
Percentage of young people running away by ethnic origin

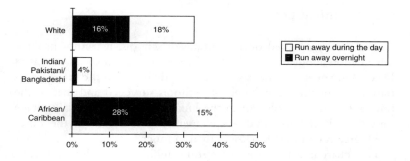

The rate of running away is far higher than average amongst young people of African/Caribbean origin, and very low amongst young people of Indian/Pakistani/Bangladeshi origin. The differences between the three groups are so large that, even with the small sub-sample sizes for two of the groups, the results are statistically significant. The results therefore suggest that African/ Caribbean young people are over-represented amongst young people who run away from home, and young people of Indian/Pakistani/ Bangladeshi origin are under-represented.

Abrahams and Mungall (1992) found a similar pattern for a sample of young people reported missing in London, and suggested that the explanation of the higher rate of running away amongst African/Caribbean young people was that the African/Caribbean population lived in economically disadvantaged areas where there were higher rates of running away in general. As shown earlier, the schools survey finds links between the economic status of families and the rate of running away and this could be a partial explanation of the differences between ethnic groups[3]. On the other hand it is also true that the Indian/Pakistani/Bangladeshi population in Leeds is concentrated in economically disadvantaged areas[4] and the rate of running away for this group is much lower than the average. In fact the 1% of young people of Indian/Pakistani/Bangladeshi origin who had run away overnight is much lower than the 9% figure for all young people in the comparatively affluent outer Leeds area (see below).

Clearly, differences between rates of running away for young people of different ethnic origin cannot be satisfactorily explained purely by economic circumstances. Other factors must be involved.

Geographical area

As the survey covered only a sample of schools, it cannot provide information about the incidence of running away in specific areas of Leeds. However, comparisons can be made between the rate of running away in the eight inner city schools surveyed and that in the four outer area schools. Again the link with economic disadvantage should be borne in mind - the unemployment rate in the outer Leeds area is considerably lower than in inner Leeds[5].

This chart illustrates the interesting finding that, whilst the run-

---

[3]Unfortunately the sample is too small to compare the rates of running away amongst the different ethnic groups, taking into account economic differences

[4]For example, in the 1991 Census the unemployment rates for economically active males aged 16 and over in Leeds were 11% for people of White origin, 22% for people of Indian/Pakistani/Bangladeshi origin and 26% for people of Black-African/Caribbean origin

[5]For example, 9.5% of the young people surveyed in inner Leeds lived in families in which nobody had a paid job, compared to 2.8% of the young people in outer Leeds. This does not take into account possible variations in family size, but these are unlikely to explain such a large difference. The information is compatible with data small area statistics on unemployment from the 1981 Census which were gathered during the planning stage of the research

ning away overnight rate was much higher in inner Leeds than in outer Leeds, the rate of running away during the day only is higher in outer Leeds. This is perhaps surprising – the overall running away rates are quite close, being 32.3% for inner Leeds and 28.4% for outer Leeds. Statistical tests of this data indicate that there is insufficient evidence of a difference in the overall running away rate between the inner and outer Leeds areas. This challenges the assumption that running away is confined to particular areas of the city. The fact that running away during the day was highest in outer Leeds suggest different patterns of running away in different areas.

Figure 8
Percentage of young people running away by area

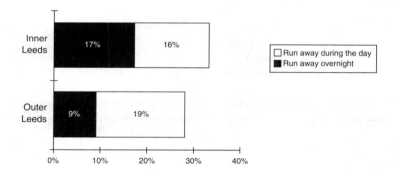

The survey sample also allows a slightly more detailed analysis of running away in different areas of the city. The schools were divided into six groups and two schools were selected at random from each group[6]. An analysis of running away rates in these six groups of schools shows a fairly high correlation between the rate of running away overnight and both unemployment and local authority housing rates. However, there is a weaker correlation in the case of overall running away rates (including day-time running). This adds further support to the possibility of different patterns of running away in different areas of the city. This issue is discussed further in Chapter 4.

---

[6]See the Appendix for details of the sampling method

School attendance

A question about school attendance was included in the survey for
two reasons. First, to examine whether there was a link between
truancy and running away. Second, to provide an indication of the
possible incidence of running away amongst young people who
weren't in school when the survey was carried out. Young people
were asked whether they stayed off school without their parent(s)
knowing. As with most of the other questions in the survey (see the
Appendix), there was a very high response rate (only 11 young people didn't answer). The distribution of answers was as follows:

Table 2
Response to the question "Do you stay off school without your parent(s)
knowing?"

Never	848
Sometimes	338
Often	37
Not answered	11

The results of this question, combined with information on running away, suggest a strong link between truancy and running away:

Figure 9
Percentage of young people running away linked to truancy

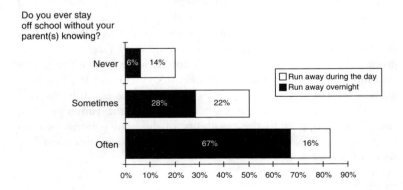

Out of the 37 young people who said they often stayed off school without their parent(s) knowing, 25 had run away overnight. This link may indicate that many of the young people who run away from their homes are also becoming detached from the education system.

CHAPTER THREE

Young people's experiences of running away

"When I was younger it didn't even really last more than a few hours, I used to get fed up straight away . . . then there was one day when I went to Blackpool and I were missing for three days. Well, once I got into the running away method I did actually run away quite a lot . . . I mean I actually got to Blackpool on several occasions, been to Accrington, Darlington, down London about four times. Then I grew out of running away unless I had real problems. This time [ie. this running away incident] it's been a month now since the last time I stayed at 'X' [Children's Home]."

The questionnaires completed in schools by young people who had run away provide an insight into differing patterns of running away – how long people run away for, where they go, where they sleep, and so on. Unless otherwise stated, the figures in this section relate only to the 174 young people who had run away and stayed away overnight.

Number of times people had run away

Most of the young people in the schools survey who had run away (67%) had done so either once or twice. 15% had run away five times or more. The average number of times a young person had run away was 2.4 times.

There are some very significant differences in the running away experiences of young people who have run away a small number of times compared with those who have run away more often (see Chapter 4).

Figure 10. Number of times young people had run away

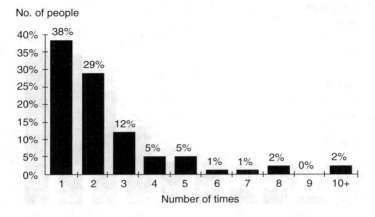

The age at which young people first run away

"I kept on running away because we had family problems you see. And I kept on running and running each day and being brought back and I was only six or seven years old. And I was running away and I was frightened and getting lost, they were finding me all over the place. I never used to reach the night in those days because I wasn't very good at it. I'd get caught during the day and I wasn't very good at staying out all night . . . and they just kept on bringing me backwards and forwards."

Figure 11 shows the ages at which young people in the survey first ran away. The average age is 12.5 years old. However the figure for 15 years of age is unreliable and the true average age is estimated as around 13 years old[1]. It is clear that the chances of running away increase as young people get older, but it is also apparent that some young people run away at a very young age – at least one in nine (11%) of the young people ran away for the first time before they were 11.

---

[1]The reason for the unreliability of the figure for the number of young people who run away for the first time at 15 is that most of the young people surveyed were some way off their 16th birthday (the average age of the sample was 15.6 years old). An unknown number of young people will have run away for the first time after they were surveyed and before they reached 16.

Figure 11. Age at which young people first ran away

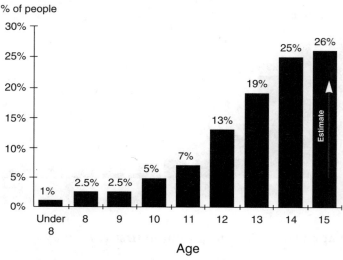

Length of time away from home

Figure 12 shows the length of time young people were away from home the last time they ran away. Just over half stayed away for one night only. At the other end of the scale, 17% had stayed away for a week or more. The fact that some young people are 'on the run' for considerable lengths of time was backed up in the in-depth interviews with young people:

> *"So I went back to 'X' [Children's Home] and I got woke up at about six in the morning. They said, 'Get your clothes and come down to the office.' I thought it was the police come for me. So I went down, sat down. She said, 'Your mum's in hospital suffering from a brain haemorrhage.' So I went to the hospital. My mam had died - she were clinically dead - she were just on the life support machine. She had two funerals, one were the cremation and the other one were scattering her ashes up at her mam's grave. I ran off after the cremation because I was so upset and I took loads of money with me 'cause my old lady used to have a bureau and it had money for the shopping and that. And I took it all and I went to Cleethorpes and I was on the run for about two months and I daren't go back because just for what they'd say for not going to the scattering of the ashes. I just didn't know what to do."*

Figure 12. Length of time away from home

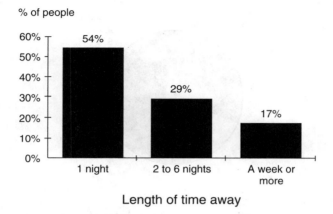

% of people

Length of time away

Running away alone

Just over half of the young people (54%) said that they were on their own the last time they ran away. However, there is a lack of clarity on this issue due to the wording of the question. The question asked was: 'Were you on your own or with somebody else?' The intention of this question was to find out if the young person had run away alone or run away with someone. During the piloting of the questionnaire it seemed that this is what young people understood by the question. However, in hindsight, the question could be interpreted as asking whether the young person was alone during the time they were away, or whether they were with someone (eg sleeping at someone's house). The 54% should therefore only be seen as a minimum figure for the number who ran away on their own: the true proportion could be much higher. The findings are not, however, at odds with the information from interviews with young people, from which it is clear that young people often run away with a friend, or in larger groups.

Where young people slept

42% of the young people who had run away overnight had slept rough the last time they ran away, making this the largest category (see Figure 13).

Figure 13. Where young people slept

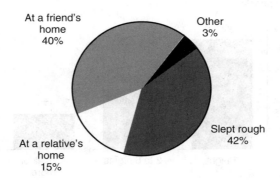

Again, this information is confirmed by the interviews with young people. Most of the young people interviewed had experience of sleeping rough. However, the kinds of places young people find to sleep are often quite out of the way. No one mentioned going to a city centre to sleep, which probably explains why the incidence of young people sleeping out is mostly hidden and very different from the traditional image of homeless adults, as these quotes from four different young people indicate:

> *"Well, I find somewhere warm first, and if I can't find somewhere warm I hide and sleep in a ditch or somewhere where there's bushes and stuff or in a wood - somewhere where I can get warm if I've got nowhere to go . . . The first time I slept out I think it was when I was 9, the first time I actually slept out on a night when I was on the run. I ran away, followed a river wharf . . . I kept on walking round because it was freezing and I went into this hut and I slept in there and I got caught - a man came in with a torch and he heard me and he took me into the house and got me a cup of tea and rang the police up and told them."*

> *"[We spent the night] in a graveyard. There were loads of us, there were lads and lasses so none of us were scared."*

> *"The first time I ran away I was five. I slept on the school playing field."*

> *"I used to sleep in this hedge in someone's back garden . . . in a plastic*

bag and when it started raining you used to have to put your head inside the plastic bag . . .it wasn't really nice 'cause there's . . . everything you know . . . loads of insects and that crawling round and you used to get really dirty . . . and then sleeping down near a bakers . . . there's a tip out the back and they put all the cardboard in there . . . so I used to just sleep in the tip . . . there's nothing dirty in it . . . it's clean, like, inside but there's loads of cardboard so you could cover yourself up under the cardboard and sleep in there."

The proportion of young people who turn to friends when they run away (40%) is also noteworthy, and consistent with information from the interviews, where friends appear as a major source of support.

Where people sought help or advice

The most important finding here is the small number of people who went to an agency for help or advice while on the run.

Figure 14. Where people went for help/advice

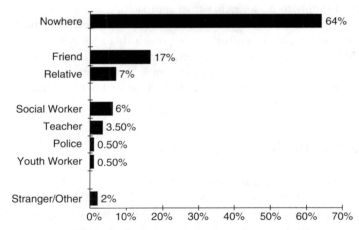

Two-thirds of the young people said that they didn't go any-where for help or advice. It is notable though, that many of the young people who slept at a friend's or relative's, did not identify these as people they went to for help or advice. This may be due to the ordering of questions on the questionnaire: the help\advice question came after the question about where the person had slept, and people may have thought they had already given information on this topic. Despite this possible confusion, it is clear that when young people do seek help or advice they are most likely to go to a friend or relative. Information from the in-depth interviews illustrates the level of support that some young people receive from friends while they are away from home. For example:

> *"I had everything I wanted really. It just depends how good your friends are to you when you run away, 'cause some of them get you food, some of them supply you with your bed, like my friends did. But, like I say, someone else might not get nowt off anyone. Like some of my mates - they're like a brother to me"*

For several reasons, it is not that surprising that few young people approach professional agencies for help or advice. First, many young people only stayed away one or two nights when they ran away. Second, young people may fear, with some justification, that if they go to the police or social services they will simply be returned home - if a young person wants to return home they may be more inclined simply to do so, rather than approaching an agency.

The interviews carried out with professionals bear out the fact that young people are unlikely to approach them for help while on the run. Most of the social workers, teachers and education welfare officers interviewed knew of young people they were involved with who had run away, but very rarely had contact with them while they were on the run.

The risks that young people face

The survey questionnaire didn't gather any information on this topic, but the interviews provide some insights into the kind of situations in which young people may find themselves. There must be particular concern in this respect for the 42% of young people who had slept rough the last time they ran away. As for the figures for the whole sample of runaways quoted above, the majority (55%) of young people who slept rough were alone and most (70%) didn't approach anyone for help/advice while they were away.

Again, those who did seek help or advice whilst sleeping rough usually approached a friend. In the interviews there are a number of examples of young people seeking support from a friend while they were sleeping out. For example:

> *"Where we live there's a lot of fields and forest. I went to a friend and he were going to sneak out and sleep out with me, you know, as company. But he didn't get to. He spoke to me from his window and I can't remember if he got caught. Well, I didn't sleep, just might have nodded off for five minutes but I were awake for all of the night, from what I can remember of it."*

In most cases, however, young people sleeping rough didn't even have the support of friends. No one should be in any doubt about the risks that young people in this situation face:

> *"I went to where I sleep rough and got my glue and sniffed until I was out of my head and then started cutting my arms like I usually do. I can't remember much else really because I was under the influence of drugs. The next morning I woke up with a man next to me, he had a bottle of vodka and some other bottles and he started trying things on with me so I punched him and kicked him and then ran off."*

What also comes across in young people's descriptions of sleeping out alone is the extreme desperation and isolation they can feel:

> *"As soon as you step onto the streets it's like you're an outsider, you're looking onto society, you're not actually involved in it any more .. that's the kind of feeling you get, you become isolated and lonely and you just feel as if no one in the world can help you. It's one of the worst feelings I've ever experienced. You just feel so unloved and uncared for and you feel as if you've got a disease and people won't kind of come near you. I've never reached that point before . . . I've wanted to kill myself before but I've never actually got that close to doing it. I just thought, 'Sod it, what's the point, nobody cares'."*

There is also evidence of young people becoming involved in high risk situations in the inner city:

> *"This pimp who I got into a car with and he tried it on with me so I ran off and the police were watching him. But he picked one lass up before and he stripped her down naked, but she won't give a statement at all*

*because she's scared that it might all come to court and she doesn't want
to stand up in court 'cause they might not believe her. He's going to pick
all the runaways up."*

A sample of 28 young people doesn't give a clear indication of
how common incidents of this kind are. However there is considerable cause for concern in the finding from the schools survey that of
the estimated 1,000 young people in Leeds who run away overnight
for the first time each year, at least 400 will end up sleeping rough.

What did people need while they were away?

This was an open-ended question on the questionnaire. 10% of
young people gave no answer at all, and 17% answered that they
didn't need anything. The answers given by the remaining 128
young people are listed below. Some people gave more than one
answer. Only answers given by three or more people are listed.

Table 3
What young people said they needed while they were away from home

Food	59	Somewhere to sleep	10
Money	50	A wash	8
Clothes	47	Toothbrush	3
Drink or water	19	Friends	3
Cigarettes	15		

As can be seen, people tended to concentrate on immediate material needs. Perhaps this reflects the reality of running away for many
young people. Young people seem usually to be unprepared for running away - lacking things like food, money and clothes. This suggests that their running away was not planned in advance. Many of
the descriptions of running away quoted throughout the report con-
firm this suggestion that many running away incidents happen on the
spur of the moment in response to a particular situation.

It does seem though, that a minority of young people plan their
running away in advance, or at least check that a friend will be willing to let them stay, before running away:

"*I couldn't stand it any more and, you know, I'd been really upset at school and everything, and my friends had been noticing it. And I'd been saying the previous day that I'd wanted to run away, but they'd been saying, 'We can't take you in.' And then the next day one of my mates said, 'My mum will take you in.' So I went home with her that night.*"

This confirms the finding in Chapter 6 that while running away is often triggered by a particular incident, there are underlying longer term issues which contribute to the young person deciding to leave.

For any running away incident of more than a day young people will clearly need food and water at least. As young people leaving on the spur of the moment are unlikely to have much money, there seem to be two options open to them to sustain themselves – either to seek the support of friends or to obtain food or the money to buy it:

"*You couldn't have no drinks of water 'cause there was nobody's house you can go to to get a drink of water, so you used to have to, like, beg money off your mates to get a 5p ice pop or something because it's got water in it.*"

The following example is from an interview which wasn't tape recorded:

"*X (aged 13) has been involved in prostitution for almost two years. At first there were many things which scared her – mainly getting into strangers' cars – now she feels less scared but doesn't enjoy it and doesn't want to do it. She rarely gets any of the money she has earned directly – her boyfriend will take it and buy her food, etc.*" [From interview notes]

These kinds of means of survival were fairly unusual amongst the young people interviewed, but they illustrate the damaging situations young people may become involved in when they run away.

Where people went

Over three-quarters (78%) of the young people stayed within Leeds the last time they ran away. The people who went outside Leeds went to the following places:

Table 4. Where young people went outside Leeds

	Number of people
Bradford	9
Other places in Yorkshire	8
Manchester	5
Other places in Lancashire	3
The North East	2
Birmingham	1
London	1
Unknown	7

This hardly fits with the image of young people seeking the 'bright lights'. Seventeen of the 29 young people who responded to the question had gone to other places in Yorkshire. Only seven young people (around 4% of the young people who had run away overnight) had gone to a large city outside the area - Manchester, Birmingham or London.

One ostensible explanation for going to other places within Yorkshire would be that young people were running to people they could stay with, perhaps relatives. However, this doesn't seem to be the case: 70% of the people who went outside Leeds also slept rough, compared with 35% of those who stayed within Leeds. The interviews with young people provide some clues to the motivations of young people who go outside Leeds. For example:

> *"I took five quid out of my brother's money box, which maybe I shouldn't have done, and I just sort of went. I went down to the station and thought, 'Where am I going to go ?', sort of thing. So I just looked up and there was a train going to Doncaster so I thought, 'I'll just go there.'"*

> *"We used to have arguments, so I just like sort of run off one day. I went to the pictures first, you know - trying to enjoy myself, and then I went to the bus station and I didn't know where to go. It was either the bus to Bradford or Wetherby, and I didn't know which one to get on, so I just got on the Wetherby one."*

According to this evidence it seems that young people may often pick somewhere to go completely at random, with the motivation of getting out of their local area, rather than being attracted to somewhere in particular.

What happened in the end?

The most common way for a running away episode to end seems to be for the young person to return home of her/his own accord:

Table 5

Length of time away from home	% of people picked up by the police
1 night	10%
2 to 6 nights	22%
A week or more	50%

There also seems to be a connection between the length of an episode and the way in which it ended:

Figure 15. What happened in the end?

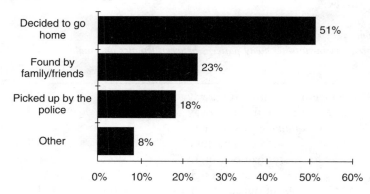

According to the findings of the survey, young people who stay away for longer periods are less likely to return home of their own accord, and much more likely to be picked up by the police. A more detailed discussion of differences of this kind is contained in Chapter 4.

No information was gathered in the survey about what happened after the episode ended - eg how parents/carers and agencies responded to the young person running away. However, this topic was covered in detail in interviews with young people, and is discussed in Chapter 7.

CHAPTER FOUR

Patterns of running away among different groups

Differences in running away between females and males

The finding that more females than males run away from home overnight was presented in Chapter 2. Table 6 presents a comparison of the different running away patterns of males and females in the survey:

Table 6
Differences in running away patterns between females and males

	Female	Male
Average no. of times run away	2.2	2.8
Average age first ran away	13	11.7
Last running away episode:		
Ran away alone	53%	55%
Away for more than one night	46%	46%
Slept rough	32%	61%
Went outside Leeds	16%	31%

The main differences to come out of this comparison are:

- On average males start to run away from home at a younger age than females
- Males are more likely to have slept rough when they run away
- Males are more likely to have gone outside Leeds while they are on the run.

There was insufficient evidence of a statistically significant difference in the average number of times males and females run away, in the proportion of males and females who ran away alone, and in the proportion who were away for more than one night.

Differences in running away according to ethnic origin

A similar analysis of different patterns of running away could in theory be carried out according to young people's ethnic origin. Chapter 2 presented significant differences in running away rates for young people of different origins, with African/Caribbean young people being more likely to have run away than white young people, and young people of Indian/Pakistani/Bangladeshi origin much less likely to have run away. Unfortunately the sample size is not sufficient to detect any further differences in patterns of running away between young people of different origins. This is because, whereas for males and females the numbers in each sub-group were both reasonably large (60 and 114 people respectively), the number of young people of non-white origin included in the 174 young people who had run away overnight is only 15. This small sub-group size is inadequate for a statistical analysis of differences to produce any significant findings.

Differences in running away between inner and outer Leeds

The professionals interviewed in the more affluent outer Leeds area were of a fairly consistent opinion that many social problems were more hidden there than in inner city areas. They had the impression that significant numbers of young people did run away in their area but that these young people were often isolated. They also felt that there were young people who, because of their isolation continued to live in intolerable situations rather than running away.

Chapter 2 shows that, whilst running away rates are higher in the inner city areas, there is evidence of a significant level of running away in the outer areas: 16% of young people in inner Leeds had run away overnight, compared to 9% in outer Leeds; for running away during the day the differences were reversed - 19% of young people had run away during the day in outer Leeds, compared to 15% in inner Leeds. The overall running away rate was therefore not that different in the two areas: 31.5% in inner Leeds and 28% in outer Leeds. These statistics are open to several interpretations. It is possible that many of the incidents of running away in the day are fairly minor, and not any cause for concern. On the other hand, it could be that young people who run away in the day in outer Leeds return home before the night because they are more isolated and have less options of where to go than young people in inner Leeds. This would tie in with the viewpoint of the professionals outlined above. Detailed research in the outer Leeds area would be necessary to clarify this issue fully. However the survey data provides some clues from comparing data for inner and outer Leeds.

Unfortunately, to a certain extent, a comparison of running away patterns in inner and outer Leeds is hampered by the sample size – only 33 of the young people who had run away overnight lived in the outer Leeds area. This makes it unlikely that statistically significant differences will emerge. The main findings are as follows:

- The average age of young people running away is very similar for the two areas
- The average number of times young people had run away is also very similar
- 69% of young people who ran away overnight in outer Leeds only stayed away for one night, compared to 50% of those in inner Leeds
- 49% of young people in outer Leeds slept rough the last time they ran away, compared to 45% in inner Leeds
- 64% of young people in outer Leeds were on their own the last time they ran away, compared to 51% in inner Leeds.

The only statistically significant difference here is that young people in outer Leeds are less likely to stay away for more than one night. However there is some evidence to suggest that, if anything, young people in outer Leeds are more likely to sleep rough, and more likely to be alone, when they run away. None of this evidence therefore contradicts the opinions of professionals working with young people in the outer Leeds area.

Developing patterns of running away

Finally in this section we consider whether there is evidence from the schools survey that there are differences in running away patterns according to the number of times young people have run away. For example, are young people who have run away most often also most likely to have slept rough?

For this analysis the group of young people in the schools survey who had run away overnight has been split into three sub-groups - those who had only run away once (66 young people), those who had run away two or three times (71 young people) and those who had run away four times or more (34 young people):

Table 7
Running away patterns according to the number of times young people had run away

| | Number of times run away | | |
	Once	2/3 times	4 times or more
Average age first ran away	13.3	12.6	11.4
Last running away episode:			
Ran away alone	47%	60%	53%
Away for more than one night	25%	49%	81%
Slept rough	25%	49%	64%
Went outside Leeds	10%	27%	31%

The main points of this analysis are:

- Not surprisingly, there is a relationship between the age at which a young person first ran away and the number of times she/he had run away. People who had run away more times had also, on average, started to run away at a younger age
- In terms of the last time the young person ran away, the three significant differences are that young people who had run away more times were more likely to stay away more than one night, more likely to have slept rough, and more likely to have gone outside Leeds.

Analysis did not find evidence of a link between the number of times a young person ran away and family background (i.e. family constitution, housing type, and unemployment).

CHAPTER FIVE

Running away from residential care

The statistical findings presented in Chapters 1 to 4 come from the survey of young people in schools. This survey, as expected, covered only a small number of young people currently living in residential care (only 8 young people out of 1,234, or 0.6%). However, 48 young people (4%) had been in care at some point, and more than half of these young people had run away overnight (not necessarily while they were in care). For this reason, and because running away from care has been such a focus of media attention and previous research, a separate survey was carried out in a representative sample of nine children's homes in Leeds.

General background

Young people living in residential care are a very small group in the total population of young people. For example, in 1991 in England the rate per 1000 young people aged 0–17 who were in care was 5.5 (i.e. 0.55%) and more than half (58%) of these young people were boarded out in foster homes, rather than in residential care[1]. Therefore, however high the running away rate from residential care may prove to be, the *number* of young people running from care is certainly considerably lower than the *number* of young people running from home.

This point is emphasized here because there is a potential for confusion about the issue, with the higher *proportion* of young people in care running away being mistakenly translated into a higher number of young people running away from care. In addition, previous research findings have sometimes been completely misquoted in the press. For example, the following extract is from a national newspaper article.

---

[1] Source: Children in Care in England. Department of Health. 1993

36

> *"According to a recent report by the National Children's Home, 100,000 children run away every year ... Although more children run away from care than from home, the report found that 23 per cent ran from their families."*

In fact the NCH survey finding was that 70% of young people reported missing had run from their family.

The misunderstandings don't end there. Running away from residential care has rarely been viewed within the context of individual young people's lives. Furthermore various negative stereotypes have been built up about young people living in residential care. For example, the tendency to view young people running away from care as criminally motivated is illustrated in Chapter 7, and a recent survey of young people in care gives an indication of the way in which young people living in care feel stigmatized within the education system (Fletcher, 1993).

One of the results of the focus on the issue of running away from residential care has been to divert attention from the issue of young people running away from their families. Focusing on the small number of young people running from residential care tends to marginalize the whole issue of running away. Blame then tends to become attached to young people in care, to the professionals caring for them, and to the 'care system' in general. Instead, the findings from this research demonstrate that running away is primarily an issue which springs from young people's experience of family life. Failure to recognize this will result in failure to tackle the real issues.

Previous research findings on running away from residential care

Abrahams and Mungall (1992) found the number of reported missing people from residential care in a twelve month period in 1989 and 1990 to be between 260 per 1,000 and 571 per 1,000 depending on area - these figures compare with rates between two and six per 1,000 for young people reported missing by families. This is very strong evidence that rates of running away from care are significantly higher than rates of running away from the family home, but may not in fact accurately reflect the relative rates for the two groups. As explained in Chapter 1, the differences are likely to be overemphasised by the survey method used in that research because the survey was based on reported missing persons. There is good reason to believe that the likelihood of an incident being reported is much higher for young people in residential care than for young people living with family. Abrahams and Mungall also found that young people running from residential care were more likely to run away repeatedly and, on average, stayed away longer than young people running from home.

Findings of the residential care survey

The residential care survey covered half of the children's homes in Leeds. The homes were selected in order to obtain a representative sample of young people aged 10 and over in residential care (see the Appendix for details). 35 questionnaires out of a possible 51 were returned – a response rate of 69%. Due to the response rate and the small sample size the findings are only tentative and should be viewed with caution. They are presented here for two reasons. First, this data is extremely rare and provides some useful tentative indicators. Second, when used in conjunction with the schools survey data, the sample size is sufficiently large to enable comparisons to be made between young people running from family and from residential care.

Rates of running away

Out of the 35 young people surveyed in residential care 28 (80%) had run away overnight, and a further 8% had run away during the day only. The margins of error on the 80% figure are plus or minus 10% (due to the small sample size). Nevertheless, this supports previous research findings that there is a far higher rate of running away amongst young people in residential care, than amongst those living with their family.

It is vital that running away from residential care is viewed within the context of young people's lives, however. For example, of the 28 young people who had run away overnight, 27 had run from residential care at some point, 20 from their family at some point, and eight had also run from foster care. Furthermore, 17 of the 28 young people (61%) said they had first run away from their family. This finding is not conclusive as the sample size is small. It is however supported by monitoring at Leeds Safe House (a refuge for young people in Leeds) which found that, over a two year period, almost three-quarters of young people from residential care had first run away from their family. The implication of these figures is that, even for young people running from residential care, the roots of running away are most commonly to be found in the period when they lived with their family.

Differences in running away experiences from home and care

The running away experiences of young people from residential care are here contrasted with those of young people running from families. The samples obtained by the two surveys are quite closely comparable with regard to age and gender - the average age for both samples was 14.8 years old, and there was no significant difference in the proportions of males and females covered. The only noticeable difference was a higher representation of African-Caribbean young people (four out of 35) in the care survey. This may be due to their over-representation in the care population.

As well as being more likely to have run away, young people who have lived in care have, on average, run away more times than young people who have run away but have never been in care (see Figure 16 on following page). Figure 16 illustrates the large difference in the average number of running away incidents between young people who had lived in care and those who had not. Over a third (36%) of those who had lived in care had run away ten times or more, but none of those young people in the schools survey who had never been in care had run away this many times. In the middle range - between three and nine running away incidents - the two groups are closer. At the other end of the scale, 43% of those young runaways who had never lived in care had only run away once, compared to 7% of those who had lived in care. These differences are statistically significant.

This doesn't necessarily mean that the young people who had lived in residential care had always, or even mostly, run away from care as it has already been seen that most young people probably start running away from home (see previous page).

Figure 16
Comparison of the number of times a young person had run away, for those
who had lived in care and those who had not
[For this Figure the term 'in care' includes both residential and foster care]

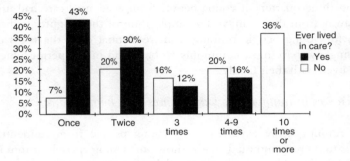

Number of times run away

A difference was also found between the ages at which young people had first run away. Those who had lived in care had first run away at an average of 11.6 years of age, compared to 12.5 years of age for those who had not lived in care. This difference is statistically significant, although perhaps not large enough to be of any practical significance.

Further major differences are to be seen in the running away experiences of young people running from care and from family. In both surveys, young people were asked a number of questions about the last time they had run away (i.e. the most recent incident). The analysis below compares those who had last run from the family to those who had last run from residential care[2]. Those who last ran away from foster care and other places were a small number and have been excluded from the analysis.

The results shown in Figure 17 are perhaps quite surprising. Young people running from their family appear to be more likely to run away alone and more likely to sleep rough than do young people from residential care. Young people running from residential care, on the other hand, are more likely to travel further afield, to

---

[2]Some of the young people in the schools survey had last run away from residential care, and similarly some of the young people in the residential care survey had last run away from their family.

stay away for longer and to be picked up by the police. These differences suggest that young people running from residential care have more support systems while they are on the run than young people running from their families, who are therefore more likely to find themselves in isolated, lonely situations. Evidently, in different ways, both groups of young people can be at considerable risk while running away. The differences in all five aspects of running away experience are statistically significant.

Figure 17
Comparison of the running away experiences of young people who had last run away from residential care with those who had last run away from their family

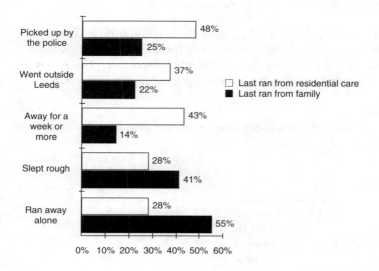

Further information from the residential care survey

The survey was designed to enable analysis of a number of other issues in relation to young people who run away from residential care. Unfortunately, due to the small sample size, a conclusive analysis is not possible. However two points emerged which raise interesting questions and may be useful for future research into running away from residential care:

1. An analysis was carried out of the relationship between the number of times a young person had run away and three indicators of their experience of living in care –

- A weak correlation was found between the number of different establishments a young person had lived in and the number of times she/he had run away[3]
- Very little evidence was found of a correlation between the age a young person first went into care and the number of times she/he had run away[4]
- There was no correlation at all between the length of time a young person had spent in care and the number of times she/he had run away[5].

It is possible, of course, that a more extensive survey would find stronger links between these variables.

2. Young people were asked their feelings about their current care placement, and (where relevant) the last time they had lived with family and the last time they had lived in foster care. The results for the 28 young people who had run away are shown in Table 8.

Table 8
Feelings about different accommodation amongst young people in residential care who had run away

	Current children's home	Last time lived with family★	Last foster placement★
I really like(d) it	8	8	4
It was/is OK	18	7	4
I am/was unhappy most of the time	2	10	6

★ Three of the young people could not remember living with their family, and only 14 out of the 28 had lived in foster care

Only 2 of the 28 young people (7%) said they were unhappy most of the time in their current residential care placement, com-

---

[3]Spearman's rho = 0.378, significance = 0.025
[4]Spearman's rho = 0.1645, significance = 0.345
[5]Spearman's rho = -0.01, significance = 0.955

pared to 10 out of 25 (40%) who had been unhappy most of the time when they last lived with their family, and 6 out of 14 (43%) who had been unhappy most of the time when they last lived in foster care. Thus their current residential care placement did not seem to evoke such strong negative feelings for these young people as did their memory of living with their family or in foster care. Clearly, such a small sample can hardly provide conclusive evidence on this issue. Nevertheless the results are interesting and suggest the need to approach the issue of running away amongst young people in residential care without preconceptions.

CHAPTER 6

Why do young people run away?

Perhaps the most obvious and fundamental question about running away is: Why do young people run away? This question is also one of the most difficult to answer. An immediate 'reason' for running away may often be fairly easy to identify (e.g. an argument with parents) but this is a simplistic approach, for two reasons. First, it doesn't put the event within the context of the young person's life – there may be underlying reasons (e.g. abuse, feelings of not being cared about) for a running away incident which stretch back years into the past. Second, it does not necessarily provide an explanation of why the young person took the drastic step of leaving their home – most young people have arguments with their parents at one time or another, but only a proportion of these young people will ever run away.

It is in fact impossible to come up with a neat categorisation of reasons why young people run away, and to fit each young person into one of these categories. Therefore, young people in the schools survey weren't asked why they had run away – the survey research method was not suitable for providing a meaningful answer to this question. Instead this chapter draws on the in-depth interviews with young people, since their detailed verbal accounts are best able to capture the complex factors which lead to young people running away. The process of deciding to run away is analyzed in three stages: first, underlying reasons identified by young people are presented; second, the immediate reasons for particular running away incidents are discussed; third, young people's motivations in deciding to run away are examined.

Before going further, it is important to be clear about the validity of the interview data. The young people interviewed for the research are almost certainly not a representative cross-section of young people who run away. A detailed discussion of this issue is contained in the Appendix but, for the purposes of this section, three key points should be borne in mind:

- Most of the 28 young people interviewed had run away on numerous occasions (between them they had run away at least 200 times) whereas, as was seen earlier, the majority of young people who run away only do so once or twice (see page xx).
- More than half of the young people interviewed (57%) had lived in residential care, compared to only 16% of the more representative sample of runaways in the schools survey.
- 26 of the young people described their ethnic origin as 'White'. Therefore the information cannot provide an understanding of the issues relevant to young Black people who run away.

Nevertheless, the high quality of the interview data (17 of the interviews were tape recorded and transcribed word for word), its rarity (young people's accounts of running away are almost non-existent in previous research in the UK), and the insights it provides, make it valuable in improving our understanding of why young people run away – and particularly those young people who run away many times. The quotes in this chapter have been numbered as some are referred to several times during the discussion.

Running away from home

Running away from family settings is dealt with first because 26 of the 28 young people had run away from their family, and in 25 cases this was the first place from which they ran away.

A: Underlying reasons

All the young people identified factors within their family which contributed towards their running away. This is an important finding in itself – indicating that the family environment plays a key role in the incidence of running away. In fact factors other than those relating to the family were hardly mentioned at all as contributing to running away. One young person seemed to indicate that problems at school were the main reason for the first time she ran away, although even here the family context can't be ignored:

"We'd just moved house and that's when it started really bad, before I

started all that again I took an overdose 'cause my dad didn't believe me when I said I were getting picked on at school, so in the end I just took an overdose and my dad believed me but it [running away] *really started when I were 12."* (Quote 1)

In all cases, the relationship between the young person and her/ his parent(s) included one or more of the following seven characteristics.

Physical violence
13 people mentioned physical violence as a factor contributing to their decision to run away, making it the most common factor. The violence described usually went far beyond punishment:

"There used to be times when my dad would crack me one, but he don't go for my legs and my arms, he goes for my head. So I think next time anybody hits me there my jaw will break 'cause it's been hit there so many times. He's knocked me out, when he slapped me once my head went bang against the cupboard, so ever since then I haven't been the same - I get dizzy spells and faint." (Quote 2)

In some cases there was seemingly constant abuse over a long period of time:

"My mam batters me and I get blamed for things. She lays into me, hits my head. She does it every day. It's been going on for eight years now. I've thought of running away before and never got the guts to do it. What got to me was when she grabbed hold of my neck. She brained me and then grabbed hold of my neck. So I went to school and didn't go home." (Quote 3)

The violence was often related to other factors discussed later in this section:

"I was living with my mum. She's an alcoholic, and I was helping to look after her and me at the same time, like look after the house, do the cooking, clean up, and I was doing meals for my mum and, you know, stuff like washing clothes, but at the same time I had to go to school as well. Then my mother started hitting me, 'cause she went through a really bad period, she relapsed and she started getting really violent. One day I thought well, you know, I've really had it - I did have a social

worker who was supposed to come and see me but she never came for ages, so I was virtually on my own. So then one day I ran away." (Quote 4)

Clearly, for this young person, who was 12 years old at the time, the violence cannot be separated from the pressure, responsibility and isolation of his situation.

The quotes also show that the violence experienced by young people cannot only be attributed to males. Fathers, mothers, step-parents and other relatives were all commonly cited as perpetrators of violence towards the young person. Additionally some young people spoke of violent relationships between their parents.

Sexual abuse

Four of the young people disclosed that they had been sexually abused by a member of their family, although in only two cases was it seen by the young person as a factor leading to running away. However it is important to bear in mind here that this information was gathered in one-off interviews where young people may not have been willing to make a disclosure of sexual abuse.

Emotional abuse and neglect

After physical violence, emotional abuse and neglect were the most common characteristics of the young people's relationships with their parents. This category covers a variety of issues. In some cases young people talked about specific incidents of emotional abuse, and a number of these incidents were related to the absence of one of the birth parents:

"They [mother and stepfather] *would start insulting my dad, who I didn't know too much about, so that upset me. And they called me a bastard which really would upset me 'cause I am a bastard you see because my mother and father weren't married when they had me."* (Quote 5)

One young person who had been adopted spoke of the following incident:

"Dad [the adoptive father] *turned round and said, 'Your mother* [the birth mother] *is the biggest slag, slut, prostitute in the whole of England and you're just like her. I want you to see your mother, if this is the*

*way you can repay us looking after you all these years then you can go to
your mother and you can have each other again.'"* (Quote 6)

In other cases there was a breakdown in the young person's relationship with his or her parents, as in the following example of a
young person who was 13 at the time:

*"... my dad pushing me about, arguing, me and my mum arguing, me
and my mum's boyfriend arguing, basically 'cause I can't get on with any
of them. They separated and my mum kicked me out 'cause she couldn't
cope with me."* (Quote 7)

Power struggles with parents

Some young people's home situations were typified by parents trying to exert very tight control and discipline. This would lead
young people to feel that their parents were failing to recognize that
they were maturing and becoming a person in their own right.
Power struggles of this nature are, of course, a feature of many
young people's relationships with their parents. However, for the
young people interviewed they were never the only significant
characteristic of the situation - they usually went hand in hand with
emotional abuse and/or physical violence, as for the following 15
year old young woman:

*"I'd been getting grounded for stupid things like not washing the plates,
and they'd been going through my stuff, opening letters that were
addressed to me and not giving me them, and my dad started hitting me,
knocking me around a bit .. To my dad I'll always be his little baby and
I'll never do anything wrong, but when it does go wrong there is a lot of
trouble. I mean if I hadn't done something wrong I'd be 18 or 19 and
still getting grounded for stupid little things and they'll be opening my
mail."* (Quote 8)

Sources of conflict included issues such as coming in times and
parental attempts to choose the young person's friends. One important category of power struggles was between young people and
stepfathers. One young man of 15 offered insights into the dynamics
within his family:

"It all started when I was six, when my mum remarried and I didn't

accept him and it just started from there. It just started like a little wall and then grew and grew and eventually it got too high so I couldn't climb over it. I mean he's a good bloke and I've got nowt against him .. but I sort of winded him up and he winded me up, so if he winded me up then I winded him up, and it were just like a little circle or a triangle or whatever you want to put it, and my mum just happened to be in the middle of it, 'cause my mum loves both of us you see, so it were hard for her." (Quote 9)

Differential treatment of siblings

Young people feeling that they were treated differently to their brothers and sisters is a theme that came up in four of the interviews and has also been identified in US research into running away (e.g. Ek and Steelman, 1988). It was never the only one of the seven characteristics present in the young person's situation, but it contributed to their feelings of mistreatment:

"It's me and my baby sister that get hit. I'm never allowed out either, but my brothers and sisters are." (Quote 10)

Too much responsibility

Another factor mentioned by four young people was a feeling that they were being given an inordinate amount of responsibility - sometimes reversing the usual roles in the parent–child relationship. One example of this has already been provided earlier in the section (quote 4). Another young person ran away for the first time at 13 primarily due to pressure at home:

"I was getting under a lot of pressure so I ran away from home for a few weeks and stayed with various friends. I felt when there was an argument I had to jump in and try and stop it. Say he's [father] having an argument with a neighbour, everyone shouts for me, and I don't see why they should treat me as the head of the house. They turn to me like I'm the man of the house." (Quote 11)

Concern about parents' alcohol use

Parents' alcohol use is not a relationship issue, but nevertheless was significant in some young people's decision to run away. In two cases it was directly linked with physical violence. For one young person there was a fear of something happening:

"I ran away 'cause my mum were drinking and I didn't want her drinking in case she did anything wrong to my brother or me." (Quote 12)

This completes the consideration of the main characteristics of the relationships between parents and the young people interviewed who had run away from home. In most cases more than one of the above characteristics was present, and in some cases as many as four. Thus all the young people who had run away from family were experiencing difficulties of one kind or another in the family setting, which in most cases included forms of physical and/or sexual and/or emotional abuse. It is notable that all these forms of abuse, together with the control and discipline issues, are indicative of the power relationship that exist between adults and children. Ultimately all these issues are rooted in the relative powerlessness of young people in our society in general, and of this group of young people in particular. This issue is discussed more fully in the conclusion.

B: Immediate reasons for running away

Young people running away from their family were often able to identify the immediate reasons for running away on a particular occasion. As some of the above quotes illustrate, in many cases there was a specific incident - an argument or instance of physical violence - which brought about their decision to run away. These incidents appear to have been the 'final straw' when added to the underlying reasons discussed in the previous sub-section. For example, one young person had suffered physical abuse from his stepfather for four years before he first ran away:

"I had an argument with my mam, I can't remember what I had an argument over. My mam says to me, 'Wait until your dad gets home,' which is my stepdad. So I thought, 'I aren't waiting till he gets home,' so I took five quid out of my brother's money box, which maybe I shouldn't have done, and I just sort of went." (Quote 13)

Not all the incidents led the young person to immediately leave home, however. Some young people waited for an opportunity - for example, two cases of young people going to school and then not returning home have already been presented (see quote 3 above).

C: Motivations for running away

The reasons for running away given in the last two sub-sections give an indication of the immediate and long-term pressures on young people which led them to decide to run away. However, there still remains the question of why young people decide to run away. The interviews indicate that there may be several different motivations for running away.

Escape
Escape appears to be the most common motivation for young people running away from their family. A phrase that kept cropping up during the interviews was 'I just couldn't cope with it any more'. This motivation is highly correlated with cases where physical or sexual abuse are involved. Often, young people who were escaping had no plan of where to go and made very little preparation. They were fleeing from a long-standing situation which had become intolerable, for example:

> *"Everything had just come to a head and my dad was trying to get rid of me and my dad were beating me up and everything and .. I just couldn't stand it."* (Quote 14)

Running to something or someone
In addition to escaping a situation, some young people had a definite place in mind where they wanted to go. For one very young person (at the age of five) it was a fair. In other cases they wanted to go to an adult who the young person trusted and who they felt would treat them better. This person could be a relative or a friend's parent. One young person (not tape recorded) regularly ran away to a friend's house. The friend's mother never turned him away and was willing to accept him permanently. He trusted her because, unlike his mother, he could talk to her and she would listen. He was not allowed to live there, and he felt that it hadn't been recognized that he was making a positive choice - he was running to somewhere as well as running away from somewhere.

Running away in the hope of changing something
At least five of the young people interviewed had hoped that the act of running away would make people take notice of their situation and therefore lead to a positive change, for example:

"I was hoping that my mum would stop drinking but she didn't."
(Quote 15)

"Every time there was a problem mum kept saying, 'Don't go, come back and we'll sort it out,' and it went right for about two or three days and then it just went wrong again. The first few times I thought it would sort itself out and then I must have realized that it wasn't going to sort itself out, that I wasn't prepared for it to go on any longer and that it needed sorting out. And I needed help with that, I couldn't do it on my own." (Quote 16)

"It were since my sister were born .. I started to get really jealous 'cause she used to get all the attention and that, so I started running away, hoping it would just bring the attention to me, but it wouldn't." (Quote 17)

As can be seen from the above quotes, these young people were often disappointed. However this disappointment did not seem to deter them from running away on subsequent occasions.

Helping friends
Interestingly, two of the young people described their first running away experience in a similar way:

"The first time I ran away, I ran away with a friend 'cause they had problems at home. I wanted to run away for them to be safe, but I didn't want to run away to worry my parents. So I went home but they started calling me names so I ran off." (Quote 18)

"This lass, she come and knocked me up one morning and said her mum's lecturing her over her new boyfriend, this that and the other, and she says, 'Are you coming on the run,'. So I says, 'No, I aren't coming.' She says, 'Oh, come on.' She twisted my arm." Interviewer: *"So that was really 'cause your friend asked you to, that you did that?"* *"Yeah and 'cause I was having troubles at home .. arguments."* (Quote 19)

It is not clear how representative this is, but in view of the large proportion of people who run off with someone (see Chapter 3), it seems likely that this kind of incident is fairly common. In both of the cases just quoted, the young person interviewed was unhappy with their own situation, as well as wanting to help out their friend.

Running away or being forced to leave ?
As young people became older there is evidence that, rather than running away from home, they were often being forced to leave by their family. Seven young people described incidents where they were forced to leave, for example:

> *"Everything had just come to a head and my dad was trying to get rid of me and beating me up and everything and I just couldn't stand it. He took me to Social Services and just dumped me. He went, 'You take care of her.' So I went to my best mates. Then he [the father] came saying, 'I want her back, I didn't mean it', and then two weeks later he did it again, except this time he said to me, 'Right we're going to beat you up and then take you down, and then they'll take you, 'cause you'll be beaten up.'"* (Quote 20)

and in another case:

> *"The reason I got kicked out of the house before was this bloke, some-body had slit one of his tyres and the police come round to all young lads my age and said to the parents, 'We can't prove your son's done it, but we think he's done it, and if it happens again we'll be coming round.' My parents went [to me], 'Oh get out.' I had to go and stay with my friends for about two weeks. I got kicked out this time the same as the first two [times]. I rang up saying, 'Well what's happened ?' They said, 'Well we don't want you back.' I said 'Fair enough. I'll sort myself out.'"* (Quote 21)

What distinguishes these incidents is that the young people were slightly older - usually aged either 14 or 15 at the time. Further-more, these young people were generally the ones who had little experience of running away. Five of them had run away only once or twice, and none had run away before the age of 12. Clearly the term 'running away' is not an adequate description of the situations faced by many young people under 16 who are away from home. In studies in other countries, various terms have been employed to dis-tinguish between different sub-groups of young people who are away from their usual homes. For example, a number of writers (e.g. Hier *et al.* 1990) have used the (perhaps dubious) term 'throwaway' to describe young people who have been forced to leave their homes. There does appear to be a need for a better developed terminology in the UK to distinguish between different groups of young people, but whatever terms are used it is a major cause of concern that young people are being forced to leave home by their families at such a young age.

Running away from residential care

A: Underlying reasons

As was stated in the introduction to this chapter, all but one of the young people who had lived in care, had run away first from their family. Consequently two points should be borne in mind throughout this section. First, the issues discussed below should be viewed within the context of the young person's life. The effect is often cumulative: whereby the factors relating specifically to the young person's time in care are added to the mistreatment the young person experienced before going into care. Second, the young person will already have had some experience of running away, and will be living with other young people in care the majority of whom also have run away. The potential for further running away must surely be much higher in this situation than it would be for a young person on their own.

The main underlying factors unique to young people in care were as follows.

The process of being taken into care

The process of being taken into care was usually viewed by the young person as being outside their control. This assessment was generally realistic, for example:

> "They put me on an interim care order and then they put me on a full care order. First it were a place of safety order because I kept running off, and they got it 'cause I was 'beyond parental control' as they says. Then they just took me into care. I met a lot of nice people but I still regret it 'cause you don't get a chance once you've been in care - no-one gives you a chance." (Quote 22)

In fact, being taken into care can feel like a punishment:

> *"I were getting beaten up by my stepdad, I was getting loads of hassle off him. I just felt like it were my fault, you know, and I were being punished, especially being put into X. Like my stepdad were allowed to live the life he wanted and I were locked up in X most of the time. It felt like I'd done something wrong by running away."* (Quote 23)

Negative experiences of the care 'system'
Often the initial negative feelings young people have of being taken into care are compounded by young people's feelings of powerlessness once they are in care, as in quote 22 above, and the following quote:

> *"Being in the care system it just like crushes you, you know, social workers that don't listen and all these rules and regulations and the bureaucracy and the red tape that you're all tangled up in, it was really really bad .. it's just like a big vicious circle that keeps going round and round and once you get caught up in it, in this big spiral, there's just no way of getting out."* (Quote 24)

Not wanting to be in care
Negative feelings about being taken into care often seemed to lead young people to feel that they shouldn't be there. This in turn could lead to young people running away from their care placement. For example:

> *"Why I run away, it's because I never get to see my family or friends half of the time; because sometimes I get bullied and picked on. But I wish it could be alright for me because if I went back home everything would be OK. While I'm in 'X' [Children's home] I always get upset. That is why I run away all the time.'* (Quote 25) (Comments written by a young person on a questionnaire)

There are also other issues in the above quote – in particular, bullying is dealt with later in this section. Nevertheless, a key factor seems to be the young person's wish to live with their family. Unfortunately, in this case, there is no way of knowing what events led to the young person being in care in the first place. It is likely that in cases such as this the incidence of running away will be to a great extent independent of the quality of care provided to the young person in the children's home.

Treatment by staff

Only two incidences of physical violence by staff were mentioned during the interviews. Thus physical abuse from staff does not seem to be as significant an issue for young people in care as it is for young people running away from their family. However relationships between the young people and staff often appear to have been poor, and this played a part in running away incidents. One young person, for example, gave her reasons for running away from care as 'the place is filthy and the staff just ignore you'. Another described how she would make sure she was listened to by staff:

> "Something had gone missing out of my room and I'd been telling them for ages to sort my lock out, and they wouldn't listen to me so I banged my hand against a wire glass window and I knew it wouldn't break 'cause I kept on banging my hand and all I got were a big crack up the window and I totally bust up my wrist so she listened to me then."
> (Quote 26)

This feeling of being ignored or not listened to is common amongst young people who run away and, as discussed in Chapter 7, doesn't just apply to young people's experience of residential care staff. Moreover, it is important to view the relationship between young people and staff within the context of young people's lives, and also to take into account the conditions in which staff work. It has already been established that most of the young people interviewed who had run away from residential care had also run away from home before coming into care. These young people had often suffered abuse within their family, and could therefore find it difficult to have trusting relationships with adults. It has also been established that these young people often came into care without being consulted and felt that being taken into care was a form of punishment. Meanwhile the staff who are given the task of caring for these damaged young people are working under considerable stress in a system where the demand for resources is often greater than the supply, and where adequate training has not always been provided (*Warner et al.*, 1992). Given these circumstances it is hardly surprising that there is tension in the relationships between children and staff in residential care. This is not said to marginalize young people's experiences and feelings, but rather to attempt to put the issue into context.

Peer pressure

A young person moving into a children's home for the first time is suddenly confronted with a whole new group of peers with whom to try to form relationships, at the same time as they have been uprooted from their family and familiar surroundings. In such a situation it is understandable that there must be considerable pressure to conform to the expectations and norms of the peer group. Running away appears to have become a part of the culture of living in care, a way of earning positive regard from other young people, and the pressure to run away (and also often to become involved in offending) appears to be very strong:

> "It's like people you meet in 'X', they get you into worse stuff, like you can't really say no because you've got to live with them .. and if you don't do what they do you get loads of hassle, so you have to be better than they are, like to prove yourself." (Quote 27)

It is perhaps significant that the above quote relates to a large children's home. The level of pressure exerted by other young people in this kind of environment may be much greater than in a small group home. For example one young person who had first run away from home at the age of six, and subsequently on many occasions from a number of care placements, went into a small group home (his seventh care placement) at the age of 15 and didn't run away from there. When asked why this was, this is how he responded:

> "Why? Because I weren't round people who were kind of asking me to go off all the time to do offences. It were all kind of for people who'd just come from broken families and they didn't know the first meaning of offending, so I was just kind of sorted .. if I'd been put in a family group home from the word go, instead of places like X where I picked everything up, I wouldn't have been offending all the time. I don't think I'd even have been to prison now." (Quote 28)

Bullying by young people

For young people in residential care, bullying was a very common factor mentioned as contributing to them running away. Again it comes up more in relation to large homes:

"They're not into sorting stuff out in them big homes 'cause if they do they just get hassle off the kids and then the others get battered for grassing on them, and then you have to do more about that." (Quote 29)

For one young person, bullying, running off, being returned and bullied further had become a vicious circle of punishment:

"Sometimes you'd run off when you were off up to the main block for your tea. Then there were always a big hard group of kids that used to run after you, beat you up and bring you back and say you fell, and the staff used to let them off, which encouraged kids to run after them and beat them up." (Quote 30)

For some young people in care the above factors, and some of the factors discussed under 'Running away from home' build up in combination over a long period of time to produce a persistent pattern of running away. Quotes from one young person, listed chronologically, illustrate some of the main themes and how these themes are inter-related:

Within 2 years of being taken into care due to physical abuse at age 7, this young person had been returned home twice, and had been in 3 children's' homes:

"That's when I started running from care - started knocking school, hopping trains and going to York without paying, Doncaster, places like that, having the day out. So they got fed up of it because one time there were loads of us who went."

A few months later he was moved to a fourth children's home:

"A lad called X came and I thought we're not having this - because we weren't allowed to go out. So we tried to walk to Leeds which was a long way. The first time we got caught, a few days later we went again and we got caught. And they had a punishment called 'the tower' - they had this sort of dark-room it was called the 'boot cupboard' in the tower and they put you in and kicked shit out of you.
"Then me and X were always going out, committing crime, that's when my offending really started - burgling every day, selling the stuff, drinking. And I was only 10 and I were drinking and everything, just because I wanted to be with the crowd and I didn't want to be left out.

".. and we went to court and I got fined and so did he and we got taken back to the children's home. That was the gist of what we were doing all the time - going out, running off, offending. Then I got into glue sniffing 'cause I wanted to be with the crowd again."

And a year later (11 years of age):

"At that time I used to take overdoses because I were really pissed off with my life in care, the old man and my mum wouldn't come and see me, I wasn't allowed home. I was the lowest I could be ever. So they put me in X Hospital which is for nutters. They put me in there for 2 weeks. Then it were again offending, I got taken to court a few times, care orders, scrubs, conditional discharges, all sorts." (Quote 33)

There are a number of themes here which also came up in other interviews:

- Running away beginning before the young person moves into care and being the result of abuse within the family
- Young people being kept in and denied freedom
- Peer pressure - wanting to be 'in with the crowd' and running away in groups
- Punishment for running away by care staff
- Rejection by parents
- Links with offending
- A number of moves within the care system and being passed from one system to another (e.g. social services to psychiatric unit to criminal justice system).

It would be misleading, however, to see this as a 'typical' example of running from care. In particular, there is a danger of labelling young people running from care as offenders. In fact, it is evident that young people also run away from care in order to avoid becoming involved in offending, and that this is another aspect of the peer pressure that can be experienced by young people living in residential care, for example:

"I was in 'X' when it was a big kid's home, they (other young people) used to like influence us to go out and TWOC and glue sniff and all

*that crud, and I didn't want to get in with them, so I wanted to get out
of that situation and get into a more friendly environment"* (Quote 32)

B: Immediate reasons for running away

Whilst analysis of the interviews with young people who have lived
in residential care has enabled the above description of the underlying factors contributing to young people's decisions to run away, it
is far more difficult to identify immediate reasons for many of the
running away incidents. Some instances where a particular sanction
or incident led to the young person deciding to run away have
already been quoted. However, in most cases young people were
not able to pinpoint specific immediate reasons for the occasions
when they had run away. It is possible that often there are no
immediate 'reasons' from the young person's point of view. The
combination of the underlying reasons and the fact that running
away seems to have become so commonplace in some residential
establishments may mean that a trigger for running away is not
needed in the way that it seems to be for young people running
away from their family. It is also clear from discussions with residential care staff that many 'running away' incidents begin when
young person fail to return to the home. This is another example of
how the term 'running away' is inadequate in describing young
people's situations.

C: Motivations for running away

Some of the common motivations for running away from residential
care were relatively uncommon amongst young people running
from their family. In particular, the desire for peer group acceptance
was common, and is illustrated by quotes 27 and 28 above.
There also appeared to be somewhat more emphasis on the experience of running away being a factor for some of the young people
in care. For example, one young person first ran away at the age of
seven:

*"I only went for the fun of it, 'cause I used to just like running away
'cause I never got my freedom."* (Quote 31)

This is perhaps closest to the stereotype of young people running away for excitement, but even here the underlying reasons that contributed to the young person running away are more complex. Elsewhere in the interview she talked of how she felt about being taken into care at the age of seven: 'Social services have never been any help to me, they put me in care and they shouldn't have done'; of her feelings about being in care: 'the staff boss you around, and put your parents down'; and the reasons why she had run on other occasions: 'we ran off 'cause we were getting loads of stick off the other kids'.

In many cases the motivations for running away were quite similar to those already described for young people running from family: escape, running to something, and trying to solve a problem. In cases of bullying, for example, running away was a means of escape. In other cases, particularly where the young person had a strong resentment to being in care, there were instances of running to somewhere that they would rather live. Finally, some young people hoped that running away would lead to a solution to a problem, or a change of placement:

"When I've got problems I might run off so then people might think 'Well if he's running off there must be a problem what needs sorting out' and people start to listen more." (Quote 34)

"When I ran away to the Safe House and then went to foster parents I thought it was the best thing for me. But now I know I'm better where I started off, at 'X' Children's Home." (Quote 35)

The variety of underlying reasons, and motivations for running away from residential care indicate the complexity of the issue. More research is needed to gain a full understanding of the issue. Nevertheless, the above analysis has provided some insights. First, it has illustrated the inter-connected nature of many of the issues and the need to look at young people's life experiences both in and out of care. Second, it has highlighted the dangers of generalizing about the issue, or of relying on stereotypes. Third, it has shown that many of the factors that lead young people to run away are not necessarily related to the quality of care offered in particular establishments.

Running away from foster care

Four of the young people had lived in foster care, and had all run
away from there. This small number of people does not allow a full
analysis of the reasons for running away, but can provide some indication of the variety of issues which arise, as the following quotes
from three of the young people indicate:

> *"They really cared for me did my foster parents, but like because of me
> living in X* [large children's home] *and been living on the streets all
> the time I felt I were getting too pampered and I thought it were making
> me really soft, so then I started running away from there"* (Quote 36)

> *"In my foster home I was there for 2 years on and off. My foster mum
> hit me over the head with a saucepan so I ran away. She used to batter
> me for running away."* (Quote 37)

> *"One night me and my foster mum had a big argument and she started
> to go on about her kids how they wouldn't do some of the things I'd done
> and her kids are brilliant and you know just being really bad to me ..
> and I was really upset and it was just one thing after another was hap-
> pening to me and each time it got worse, like I'd just been suspended
> from school for something I hadn't really done and all the teachers were
> being really bad to me."* (Quote 38)

Some of the reasons for running from foster care may in fact
often be no different in nature to the reasons why young people run
away from their family - incidences of physical violence and differ-
ential treatment are cited above - but there may be additional factors. As with residential care, foster parents are trying to care for
young people whose experiences have been damaging. Their previous experiences of family life have not been good, and it may be
that being fostered is too similar to these experiences for the young
person to feel comfortable.

Conclusions

The reasons why young people run away are many and varied.
Often there are multiple reasons for a running away incident.

Immediate reasons like an argument, or a violent incident, are usually only the trigger for running away, when in fact there are deep-seated longer term problems. It seems that for a young person to run away, two things are required: first, one or more factors in the young person's home/care environment which are causing them distress (often over a long period); and second, a specific motivation for running away at a certain point in time.

Most of the motivations identified above for running away (e.g. escape, trying to change something) could be described as 'push' forces, i.e. arising from features within the young person's home environment which push them into running away. These are often linked with factors such as abuse at home or bullying in care. There were some motivations (e.g. pressure from friends) which could be described as 'pull' forces, i.e. things outside the young person's home environment which encourage them to run away. However it was found that even in cases where these motivations were present, one or more of the key contributory factors indicating difficulties in the home environment were almost always present. The overall impression from the interviews conducted is that the 'push' factors carry far more weight than the 'pull' factors. Certainly, judging by this group of regular runaways, the idea that most young people run away for excitement seems to be a myth. Even in the minority of cases in the interviews where this was a factor, there was often great distress in the young person's life, from which running off provided a temporary respite.

CHAPTER 7

Adults' responses to young people who run away

This section discusses the responses of adults to young people who run away, not only during or after a runaway incident but also in dealing with the key issues affecting the young people, such as abuse. It makes use wholly of young people's accounts of adults' responses, although it is recognised that the adults involved will have had a different perspective of the situation. Each of the key groups of adults involved in young people's lives are dealt with in turn in this chapter, which uses material from the 28 in-depth interviews with young people.

Parents

In general, parents had three different kinds of responses to a young person running away. The first was a positive response, involving concern for the young person's welfare, and relief and affection when the young person was returned safely:

> "*My mother were pretty worried. She were looking all over for me. She didn't know and as I were only 12 she wondered where I might have gone, where I could be. My dad was out looking for me .. [when I got back] they cuddled me and says, 'Don't do it again you scared me', and I felt guilty that I did it.*"

Perhaps surprisingly, the above quote (which refers to the first time the young person ever ran away) is the sole example of a completely positive response from parents in any of the 28 interviews.

Slightly more common was a neutral response. The young person just quoted, for example, continued to run away, and his parents' attitude slowly changed:

> *"They just got used to it. You know, 'Oh nice to see you, welcome back.' Then eventually she [mother] stopped coming to pick me up herself. She let the police or social services bring me back. She were used to it in a way."*

However, by far the most common response was a negative one, involving either punishment or physical violence:

> *"My dad's been really nasty. He grabs you round the neck and says, 'Where the bloody hell have you been?' and locks you in your bedroom."*

Being 'grounded' was a very common form of punishment for running away. Ironically this seemed often to make the young person more determined to run away again.

It was mentioned in Chapter 6 that for some young people one of the motivations for running away was to try and draw attention to a problem and to achieve a positive change, but on reflection young people rarely felt that this had happened. In fact, running away often seemed to make things worse and lead to an escalation of conflict:

> *"They were dead angry at me. They said 'What have you been telling them?' and stuff like that. When I told them I didn't like the way they were treating me they just went, 'You should be grateful for what we've given you.' They started taking stuff off me and everything. That's about the time when they started grounding me permanently."*

Parents often also reacted with fear or anger at the thought of any outside agency becoming involved. There was a tendency to want to 'keep it in the family':

> *"All my mum keeps saying is, 'We could have sorted this problem out on our own'. I mean social services are involved now but mum's just saying 'It's nothing to do with anybody except our family' . . . they're petrified at the moment because social services have been involved. They've got the idea now that I'm not going to come home now I'm going to be in care or foster care."*

Of course, the bias in the interview sample is particularly important here. Nearly all the young people had run away more than once. It may be that there are many young people who run away once and never again, because parents react in a caring way and things improve. What the interviews illustrate is that for the minority of young people who run away a number of times the responses of parents may well be predominantly negative and punitive from the outset.

Other relatives / friends' parents

One example of a young person's sister being supportive is quoted in the next section (see page 68). Generally relatives and the parents of friends reacted positively but cautiously to young people who had run away. Often they would let the young person stay for a few nights and then encourage or persuade to return home. In other cases they let the young person stay for longer. For example, one parent of a friend offered to take a young person in permanently. From the interviewing with professionals it seems that such informal fostering arrangements are quite common. What very few of these adults appear to have done, however, was either to become involved in the issues affecting the young person or to involve the police or social services in the running away incident. In many cases therefore the young person will have run away and later returned home without the issues which led them to run away being addressed, and without any agencies being aware of the incident. In some cases a 'cooling off period' may have been all that was required, but in other cases this must be seen as a missed opportunity for an adult to help a young person to try to get some assistance with their problems.

Police

Police have a key role to play in dealing with young people who run away. They may often be the only professional agency which is involved with the young person during the running away incident. Young people's experience of the response of police to their situation was sometimes very positive, for example:

> *"I know one police officer who listens to you and that's PC 'X', and he's really got on well with me. I like him a lot."*

However, a common response seemed to be for the police to try to frighten the young person into not running away again:

> *"And then PC 'X', who's the one in charge of runaways, comes and gives you a hard time about it and says 'Do you want to be taken to where that ripper went and murdered all his victims,' so I says 'No, I don't want to,' so he just shouts at you like, 'You wouldn't want to be murdered would you ?' He really does give you a hard time and swear at you and everything and he don't believe a word you say about why you've run away … But it didn't work 'cause you know not to believe a word he says."*

> *"That copper, I hate him. He says to me the second time he found me, 'One of these days you're going to end up shagged, bagged and binned.' He says it to all the lasses, any age he wouldn't be bothered. When I got caught running before, the sergeant got all these photos out of all the kids he'd found that were, you know, dead, and I just had to walk out after one photo. It still didn't work."*

It is perhaps understandable that police offers, being acutely aware of the dangers that young people face on the streets, should try this approach. Indeed it may act as a deterrent in many cases. However, for young people who are experienced at running away, or who are fleeing abusive situations, it appears to be ineffective.

Particularly for young people running from residential care, there were instances of the young person being assumed to be a criminal. In the case below this is particularly ironic because the young person had been running away from care to avoid pressure from other young people to go on the run and commit offences:

> *"They* [the police] *just give you a lot of abuse and that, you know, 'Come here you fucking little ..' and all that. Called me a vandal and a criminal and all that. Anything that had been done in the area you'd always get asked about it, just 'cause you were from a kid's home basically. If a house had been broken into you'd be the first suspect."*

This is an example of the kind of negative labelling that young people in care face in many areas of their lives (Fletcher, 1993).

Finally many young people felt that they hadn't been listened to or taken seriously. One young person who had run away because of her mother's drinking said she had told the police why she had run away and 'they just went quiet'. Another young person, who had been sexually abused at home and had previously disclosed the abuse to police and social services, ran away and was picked up by the police:

> *"The police officer, who'd seen me before when I was 13, came in and started asking me questions and saying, 'You didn't get abused, you must be lying', and stuff like that, giving me a really hard time. And I just said, 'If you must know I did get abused.' So she said, 'Yeah well you said that before and that's what you're like.' She relates this story - 'Peter cry wolf' or something - and she says, 'You just want your freedom. You want to go home, that's the best place for you.'"*

Another young person had fled his violent mother and gone to his sister's house:

> *"My mum came over to my sister's house and she started banging on the windows and doors, and I was really scared and frightened that she'd pull me back home .. and I hid in, you know, those things under the stairs, the little cubby hole. And my mum had called the police and the police came over and this policeman searched around my sister's house and then finally he comes and he finds me and goes, 'Come on mate, come out, get out here.' So I came out and mum was sat in the living room and the copper was going on about how I should go home and all this, but I'm saying, 'Look my mum's hitting me,' but he wouldn't believe me. Luckily at that point my sister came back and she says, 'What's going on here?' and I told her. So my sister says to the policeman, 'Look, he's not leaving here, she's not in a fit state to look after him.'"*

As the following sections of this chapter will show, this tendency not to listen to what young people are saying is not unique to the police.

One further point regarding the police is that young people who run away often view them as 'the enemy' as it is the police who have the duty of looking for them and returning them home. This inevitably creates a barrier. One young person admitted that the police were 'nasty, probably 'cause I were nasty to them, told them where to go, "I'm not going home."' While police are seen as having this role it is likely that many young runaways will continue to be hostile towards them. This will present an obstacle to the development of a positive role for the police in dealing with running away.

Social workers

Most of the young people interviewed had had some involvement with social workers. Young people's feelings about social workers were quite mixed. There were a number of instances of very positive relationships with social workers:

> *"He took me places and he did my life story book. He did a lot more things for me than any other social worker has done. He got me adopted. He got me about three different kid's homes to go look at. He were ace."*

Social workers who were active on young people's behalf, and who listened to them, were viewed positively:

> *"I've had quite a few social workers. There's been a couple that have been really good and I've got on really well with but then they've all left 'cause they're sick of the system .. I can tell with someone if they listen to me or if when I'm saying something it's going in one ear and out of the other. I mean with the social workers I've had I can tell this, and just the way they talk to me and react to me, they're a lot more friendly to me, a lot more down to earth and natural, the good ones. And if I actually say that I would like something they will do all they can to try and put it into practice."*

On the other hand, a common theme was that of not being listened to. From young people's perspectives some social workers were far too ready to side with adults against them:

> *"She asked my mam if she were drinking. My mam said, 'No', and the social worker believed her."*

> *"My sister's boyfriend he were hitting me and being a real bastard to me and so I ran away and I went to stay at a friend's, then I went back the next day. When the social worker came round they were all nice to me and all that, you know, as if nothing had happened .. she [the social worker]*

wouldn't believe me, you know, it was as if she was on their side."

In these two cases the issues that the young person wasn't able to get the social worker to listen to eventually led them to run away.

Residential care staff

Young people's relationships with residential care staff, and the stresses on those relationships, have already been discussed in Chapter 6. In terms of staff's responses to running away, by far the most common response when a young person was returned was to punish them - usually by sanctions such as 'grounding'. This response can be seen as understandable in the sense that running away has become part of the 'culture' in care, but clearly there is a danger of taking running away for granted. As discussed in Chapter 6, many young people run from care because of bullying. In these cases sanctioning the young person on their return means he or she is doubly punished, while the perpetrator of the bullying is not dealt with. It may be that young people are reluctant to disclose bullying for fear of reprisals but some young people felt they hadn't been given a chance to discuss their problems on their return to care:

> *"If you're in care you've got nowhere, you can't go back unless you want a bollocking about it, or punished like grounding or stuff like that .. That's all they do. They don't speak to you, ask you why you've run away or owt like that. They just kind of go, 'That's it, you've run off, grounded for a week, extra things to do.'"*

Teachers

For most young people, teachers are the only professionals with whom they have regular contact. Teachers have the opportunity to get to know young people and may be in a good position to detect any signs of distress. Quite often it was a teacher who first noticed physical abuse and involved social services or police:

> *"In the end a teacher referred me to social services because of bruises and because of me not being able to read or write, and me freaking out when-*

ever a male teacher came into the room."

Unfortunately, some parents, aware of this possibility, kept their children home from school when they were bruised.

Of course teachers can't detect every case of distress or abuse, but it is important always to be aware of the possibility:

> *"I used to come to school crying my eyes out and they just weren't both-*
> *ered. They just used to look at you and say, 'Stop crying and get on*
> *with your work.' They just thought it were boys, 'cause I'd been going*
> *through quite a few boyfriends and stuff, so they just presumed it were*
> *that, and I didn't bother telling them they were wrong."*

There were positive examples, though, of teachers being extremely supportive of young people:

> *"They've been really great to me, especially one teacher. I mean she*
> *hasn't been through the stuff I've been through but she sort of had panic*
> *attacks, which I've had and she's been really understanding about it and*
> *supported me, so it's been great. She got me back to school after six*
> *weeks. She picked me up in the car every morning as well, which were*
> *nice. You know, you don't expect a teacher doing this. She's really*
> *nice."*

This kind of intervention can be particularly helpful because many repeated runaways have had very disrupted schooling. Data indicating a very strong relationship between running away and truancy was presented in Section 3. Interview data again support this finding. There were differences in the educational experiences of the young people who had livied in residential care and those who had not.

The young people interviewed who had run away from their family in their teenage years generally had also described a disrupted school attendance. Some seemed to have become completely alienated from the education system:

> *"School weren't very fair with me 'cause about two or three months ago I*
> *got expelled from school. I'd been getting suspended for about eight*
> *months. I'd get suspended for two weeks, I'd go back and within two*
> *days I'd get suspended for two more weeks. They wanted me out really*

and they were telling me not to come and all sorts of things like that"

However, almost all the young people with experience of the care system seemed to have lost touch with the education system. Comments like the following were common to many of the interviews with young people who had been in care:

"I've done that for two years - knocking off school - I just don't go. It was only the odd week and then I started going back. As soon as I hit care I never went .. so I haven't been since, just don't like school, gone off it. Once you get into the habit of knocking off you can't get back into the habit of going. You feel 'What's the point in going?'"

The survey and interviews therefore present a picture that, in general, young people who run away are also likely to be irregular school attenders. Nevertheless for two of the young people interviewed, one from home and one from care, school appeared to be a highly important aspect of their life.

Other agencies

Young people only rarely mentioned involvement with agencies other than those discussed above, either while they were away from home or when they returned.

Youth workers weren't mentioned at all by any of the young people interviewed. Although this is in accord with the schools survey finding that only one young runaway had sought help/advice from a youth worker while they were on the run, it is surprising that a service that is specifically aimed at young people was not used by some of the people interviewed when they were in need of help.

Three young people had tried to contact Childline. Two of these young people had been unable to get through when they had tried because the lines were busy, which is prehaps indicative of the level of demand for this kind of service. The other had hung up when she was asked for her name.

Three young people in care had been referred to psychiatric services including two who had been admitted to psychiatric hospital. Their feelings about this were fairly negative.

Finally one young person had been involved with a doctor due to a sexual abuse disclosure (see below).

Conclusion

The drawback of dealing with each key adult or agency separately as above is that there is no picture of the overall effect on particular young people's lives. To illustrate this issue, here are extracts from one young person's description of disclosing sexual abuse:

> "Since I were 13 I were getting sexually abused by my brother. I kept running away and I got a social worker and she were no good at all .. it was such a long time, I kept running away, going back home, or I just used to get taken back home, and then I did my statements at the police station, Child Abuse Team .. they were saying times and dates and I said my times and dates but then my social worker were saying that my mum and dad didn't believe me, and that my brother wouldn't do anything like that , and so I were getting it into my head that no-one believed me, so I thought, 'What's the point?' .. so next time I went to the police station to do some more statements I said some wrong times and dates, so when they checked up a police officer said to me, 'I know you're lying,' and I found out my mum were sticking up for my brother and giving him alibis, so there were no chance. I had my medical, I saw Dr.'X' and she were really nice, and the medical evidence said that I'd got sexually abused, and I were telling her, 'No-one believes me,' so she said, 'I'm going to write a report and say that medical evidence sticks by your story.' By this time the social worker were on my back all the time asking if I'm lying and stuff .. she was just really giving me a hard time."

Eventually the young person withdrew the allegations. It's hardly surprising that young people who run away often appear to have lost faith in adults:

> "I think what [young people] need is to be listened to and not to be told that they're talking a load of bullshit, 'cause that's what I've been told, you know, 'You're talking a load of bull, you're a little kid, you don't know what you're on about, we're adults we can do what we like,' and it's not right. Everybody - police, parents, teachers, social workers -

all of them's called me a liar, and said I'm telling them bullshit."

Some young people seemed to have given up hope in a positive response from adults:

> *"I was just feeling really depressed, really lonely, so like I was crying out for help and everyone just turned their back on me, you know, my teachers, my social workers, nobody wanted to know', [and later in the interview], 'I was at rock bottom .. 'cause I'd totally lost my confidence in adults completely.'"*

Young people who have lost their faith in adults in this way must be even more vulnerable to mistreatment and abuse as they are unlikely to feel there is any point in turning to anyone for help.

CONCLUSIONS

Summary of main findings

High incidence of running away:
The research indicates that running away is a sizeable problem amongst young people in Leeds. The survey of a large representative sample of young people aged 14 to 16 found that one in seven had run away and stayed away overnight before the age of 16. This is a higher incidence of running away than previous research has estimated. One possible reason for this is that the two previous studies carried out in the UK have relied on missing person statistics. The current research suggests that these statistics may be an underestimation of the incidence of young people running away from their family, although fairly accurate for those running from residential care establishments.

The widespread nature of running away:
Having established the widespread incidence of running away amongst the youth population, the report goes on to explore the characteristics of young people who run away. Running away is not restricted to one sub-section of the population of young people: young runaways may be male or female, from various family structures and economic backgrounds, from a variety of cultural backgrounds, and from all areas - urban, suburban and rural. Nevertheless some young people are more likely to run away than others: for example females are more likely to run away than males; young Asian people less likely to run away than other young people; and factors such as family structure and family economic background also seem to have an influence on the likelihood of a young person running away. There is also a strong link between truancy and running away.

A hidden problem:
The high incidence of running away found in this research will surprise many people, especially as the sight of young runaways on the

75

streets may not be common outside London. The research throws some light on this paradox. Many young people who run away end up sleeping rough, but far from gravitating towards city centres, they seem to sleep and spend their time in places where they are less likely to be found. Furthermore the majority of young people who run away do not approach any professional agencies for help while they were away, although they may seek help from friends. Thus they often go unseen by the adult population. It is significant that most of the 1,234 young people surveyed in schools had a friend who had run away. Few runaways appear to go outside their local area when they run away.

Repeated running away:
The diversity of young people who run away indicates that there would be some value in attempting to divide runaways into sub-group with similar characteristics. The precise delineation of these sub-groups is a task for future research, but one group of particular interest are the minority of young people who run away repeatedly. The surveys carried out as part of the current research indicate that this group have many characteristics which distinguish them from other young runaways. For example, they often seem to become involved in more lengthy and potentially risky running away episodes.

In-depth interviews carried out as part of the research tended to focus on young people who had run away on a number of occasions. While these young people cannot be taken as a representative sample of regular runaways, the interviews offer some indications of these young people's backgrounds, and the roots of their running away behaviour. Repeated runaways usually first ran away from their family. Their relationships with their parents are often characterised by physical, sexual or emotional abuse, and by power struggles. Their motivation for running away is often simply to escape from the abuse and mistreatment they were suffering, in fact this may be the only way that they feel they can escape the abuse. Some hope that by running away they will achieve a change in their situation, as well as gaining some respite.

Often these young people also spend time in residential care, although this normally occurs after they begin running away. In fact there is often a link between the young person starting to run away and their subsequent reception into care. In these cases running away incidents have drawn attention to the underlying factors. In general, once they are within the care system these young people continue to run away.

Running from residential care:
The research indicates that the majority of young people aged 10 and over in residential care in Leeds have run away, many of them repeatedly. This is in keeping with previous research findings. An important new finding, however, is the evidence that most young runaways from care begin running away before being taken into care. Findings from the survey of young people in care and from the interviews with young people who had lived in care indicate that this is a particularly complex issue. Whilst many of these young people may have specific problems relating to their care placement which contribute to their running away, it is vital to see their running away within the context of their lives. It is erroneous to label these young people simply as 'absconders' or 'care runaways', they have in fact often run away from wherever they have lived, including (in the first instance) their family, and subsequently both residential and foster care placements. Their life stories suggest a whole series of events, often going back to early childhood, which have contributed to their behaviour. The research therefore challenges the idea that there is an easy way to stop these young people continuing to run away. It is tempting to conclude that more preventative work is needed before young people have reached their teenage years and developed a pattern of running away.

Policy and practice implications

The research was conceived as a descriptive piece of work, rather than one which would influence specific policy. However, the information from the surveys and interviews with young people carry important messages for the development of more effective preventative strategies and responses to young people who run away.

The need to hear the young person's viewpoint:
Often the young people expressed the feeling that adults had not listened to their concerns, and that they had been returned to the place they ran from without any change in their situation. It is

hardly surprising, then, that these young people had continued to run away. Above all else, the research points to the need to understand running away within the context of a young person's life and from a young person's viewpoint. This may seem to be stating the obvious - a person's behaviour cannot be fully understood without taking into account their viewpoint. Yet the most common theme to come out of the interviews with young people was their feeling of not being listened to.

The possibility of preventative work:
Given the risks that many young people face when they run away from home, consideration must be given to the possibility of preventative work in this area. The young people interviewed often expressed the view that they may not have started running away if there was someone there they could trust, and who would listen to them. This suggests either that there is a barrier to young people making use of current services which could meet their needs or that these kind of services do not exist. An effective preventative programme should therefore have at least two components. First, the provision of an accessible service which catered for young people's needs. Some of the basic requirements of such a service would be that young people felt taken seriously, and that they felt able to trust the service. Second, information which raised awareness amongst young people about the issue of running away, and the services that were available to them.

Running away as a child protection issue:
The research cannot give an indication of the proportion of young runaways who are suffering from serious abuse or neglect. But the fact that so many young people who run away are alone, and have nowhere safe to sleep, and yet do not approach agencies for help must in itself be sufficient cause for concern. Running away is to a great extent a hidden problem, and this makes it very difficult to research. The interviews that were carried out were not truly representative, and there is no way of knowing whether the catalogue of mistreatment and abuse which these young people recounted is reflected in the overall population of runaways. However, until it is established that this is not the case, it would surely be safer to regard running away as an indicator that there may be something seriously amiss in the young person's home environment. This may require a

change of attitude on the part of professionals and other adults. It seems from young people's accounts that many of them were returned home after a running away incident without any serious attempt to establish whether this was in their best interests. It also seems that a very common response to dealing with running away is to punish the young person. This suggests that young people who run away are viewed as perpetrators of an offence, rather than victims of the actions of others. They therefore suffer in two ways – first of all by being subjected to abuse or mistreatment and then, second, by being punished for their attempts to escape or draw attention to their situation. One possibility would be for evidence of running away to be automatically considered a child protection issue and for appropriate procedures to be instigated to establish whether the young person is at risk. Area Child Protection Committees would clearly have an important role here in co-ordinating the different agencies involved.

Responses to running away:
Abrahams and Mungall (1992) have suggested that all young people reported as missing to the police should be interviewed when they return home. This would clearly be a most important step in the direction of ensuring that young people had an opportunity to discuss their situation. The key issue here is who should provide this service. Abrahams and Mungall suggested that it could be the police, social services, or some other agency. The research has given some indication of the potentially conflicting role of the police in dealing with young runaways. The police are charged with the task of attempting to locate and return young people reported as missing, and therefore, from a young person's point of view they are often seen as people to avoid while on the run. This would seem to produce a barrier to effective communication between the police and young people once they have returned home. Social workers also often have a dual role to play. In terms of young people running from families, they may already be involved with the family as a whole. There are indications from the young people interviewed that this creates difficulties in terms of the young person feeling that they have had a fair hearing. This suggests that, within the current context, it may be difficult for either the police or social workers effectively to provide a service which would cater for the needs expressed by the young people throughout this report. It may how-

ever be possible for social services to provide a service which is distinct from family casework. The option is for an independent non-statutory agency to take on the role.

The other issue that remains unresolved is how best to provide a service to those young people running from families who are not reported missing. The report suggests that, these may well be a group of young people who are particularly at risk within families. In fact this may be the reason why parents don't report their running away. The research has also found that few young runaways approach agencies while they are away from home (although it must be noted that the vast majority of running away incidents included in the survey had taken place before the opening of a refuge for young runaways in Leeds in 1991). Again the answer must lie in providing services which are accessible to these young people at any time, but especially while they are on the run. An essential part of making services accessible would be to raise young people's awareness of their existence before they run away, since young people are unlikely to find out about them while they are away from home.

The research presented in this report, and that carried out by Abrahams and Mungall, both suggest that very few young people seek the 'bright lights' when they run away from home. Nevertheless, the small minority that do go to a large city must be at considerable risk, and there is evidently a role for agencies in these cities who seek to make contact with these young people and offer them support while they are on the streets.

A more widespread issue is the way in which other adults can respond to running away. It is clear from the accounts of young people that, whilst a good proportion of the incidence of running away is hidden, in many cases adults do have contact with young people either in the period immediately preceding a running away incident or while they are away. The parents of the young person's friends, for example, will often become involved when the young person approaches friends for help and is given a place to stay for a few nights. The research indicates that these adults can play a key role in ensuring the young person's welfare, if they take seriously what the young person says and are willing to support the young person in obtaining further help if necessary.

The role of refuges:
The issues that lead young people to run away are often extremely

complex. In these cases it is likely that an immediate return home would often not be in the best interests of the young person, and that these interests could be best served by a short period away from the home environment in order to attempt to resolve the issues concerning the young person. For this reason the Children Act 1989 provided for the first time a legal framework for the provision of short term refuge to young people under 16. Refuges which are approved by the Department of Health have limited exemption from laws relating to the harbouring of young people, and are able to accommodate them (in the first instance) for a continuous period of up to 14 days. There are currently only a handful of such refuges in the country – providing at most between 20 and 25 bed spaces on any given night.

Areas for future research

Inevitably the report also suggest areas for further research. The issue of running away is still relatively unexplored in the UK and a handful of research studies cannot be expected to adequately cover such a complex topic. In particular, the report has drawn attention to the need for further research in the following areas:

● The significance of running away for young people from different cultural backgrounds, and an exploration of the apparently large differences in running away rates for young people of African-Caribbean, Asian and White origins.

● The running away experiences of young people who have lived in care. The research suggests that it would be vital for any such research to take full account of the young person's life history and their experience of running away from the family as well as the care system. It may also be illuminating to research the minority of young people in residential care who have no experience of running away.

● The reasons for running away amongst young people who only run away once or twice. This group includes the majority of runaways, but only a few were reached during the interviews. Little is currently known about how their running away may differ from that of more regular runaways.

Finally, we know very little about the impact of running away on a young person's life. For example, research in the USA (Simons

1991) suggests that many young people who run away subsequently experience homelessness as adults. A study which examined the long term effects of running away would be valuable.

APPENDIX

Research Methodology

The schools and residential care surveys

Sampling methods used

a)   *The schools survey:* The secondary schools in Leeds were divided into
six groups, on the basis of information provided by Leeds City Council Education Department and data on catchment areas extracted from
the 1981 Census.   One group was made up of units representing the
five inner Leeds schools with the highest proportions of Black pupils.
The other five groups were based upon location (inner/outer Leeds),
and on the unemployment rates and proportion of local authority
housing in the areas in which they were situated. To control the size
of the final sample some large schools were divided into two units and
some small schools were combined into one unit. Two units were
selected at random from each group. Where one of the selected
schools declined to participate in the survey a replacement unit was
randomly selected from the remainder of the units in that group. In
all, 18 schools were approached regarding the survey, of which six
chose not to participate. The 14 to 15 year old age group was surveyed in one of the schools in each group and the 15 to 16 year old
age group in the other school. It was agreed that the identity of the
schools involved would not be revealed.

Response rates in the schools varied. Almost all the young people present on the day of the survey chose to participate. However school
attendance rates varied and the average rate for the whole survey was
84%. A second run of the survey was attempted in schools where the
attendance rate had been lower than 90%, but this only produced a
small number of additional questionnaires. This suggests that often the
same pupils were absent on both occasions. The missing data can be
explained partly by random factors (e.g due to illness) which are
unlikely to have had a large overall effect on the representativeness of
the sample, and systematic factors (e.g. regular truancy) which mean
that some young people were less likely to be included in the sample.
In anticipation of this, a question about truancy had been included in
the questionnaire and, as shown in the main body of the report, evidence was found of a link between truancy and running away (see also

later). In order to reach young people who were regularly away from school, a small supplementary postal survey was attempted with the assistance of Leeds City Council Educational Welfare Service. This survey only produced a response rate of approximately 25% (20 forms out of around 80 distributed) and so the data could not be used. One of the main problems with this supplementary survey was that parental permission was required before the form was given to the young person, and parents often objected.

The final sample was made up of 1,243 completed questionnaires. Nine of these questionnaires (0.7%) were spoiled in some way and not suitable for analysis – leaving 1,234 questionnaires. The final sample consisted of 675 females (55%) and 559 males (45%) – this was due to the inclusion of three single sex schools in the sample. 74% of the young people were aged 15 – the remaining proportions were 13 years old (4%), 14 years old (15%) and 16 years old (7%). A comparison with 1991 Census data for Leeds indicates that the sampling method was effective in obtaining a representative sample of young people in terms of family consitution and economic background. It was also successful in representing the multi-cultural constitution of the population (see Table 1 in the main body of the report).

b)   *The residential care survey:* The children's homes in Leeds were split into three groups on the basis of size and function, and a proportion of homes in each group were selected. The survey was carried out in nine homes out of a total of 18. On the days surveyed these homes accommodated 51 young people aged 10 and over. All these young people were asked to fill in a questionnaire. 35 questionnaires were returned – a response rate of 69%. This response rate does raise concerns about how representative the sample is. However it was clear during the conduct of the survey that much of the missing data was due to random factors. Therefore, given the uniqueness of the data, the results have been presented in the report with a clear statement drawing attention to the extent of their validity.

Survey questionnaire formats

The schools questionnaire was drawn up after draft versions had been tested with the help of young people. Young people filled in the draft questionnaire, their understanding of the meaning of the questions was checked, and their views on the general questionnaire format were obtained. This testing resulted in a large number of improvements before the questionnaire was finalised. A similar process was followed for the residential care survey. It is not possible to reproduce the questionnaire formats in this report, due to space limitations. A copy can be obtained from the address provided at the end of the appendix.

Response rates to questions

a)   *The schools survey.* The response rates for questions were in general very good. Most questions had a completion rate of 96% or higher, but there were four exceptions. Data from two of these four questions has been omitted from the analysis in this report. The data for the other two questions relates to age at which the young person first ran away (6.9% missing) and what the young person needed while they were away (9.8%). This has been noted in the main body of the report.

b)   *The residential care survey.* Response rates were very good, with no more than two missing responses to any of the questions, with the exception of the question on what young people needed while they were away.

Statistical analysis

Where appropriate, statistical analysis of differences between sub-groups was carried out. The main tests used were the Pearson Chi-square test (for cross tabulations of categorical data) and the Wilcoxon-Mann Whitney Rank Sum test (for differences in means for interval data). Log-linear methods were used for the analysis discussed in relation to Figure 6, and Spearman's rank correlation coefficient was calculated for some ordinal data statistics as indicated in Chapters 2 and 5. In all cases where a 'statistically significant' difference is reported, these differences were found at at least the 95% confidence level (i.e. p-value < 0.05). For most of the differences in Chapter 2 where the chi-square test was used the p-values were much smaller than this (generally less than 0.001). However this is not unusual with such large sample sizes (over 1,000 in this case), so statistical significance has not been emphasized too strongly in this chapter.

The figures on proportions of young people who run away presented in Chapter 1 were estimated on the basis of the stratified cluster sample method and 95% confidence intervals have been provided on the relevant page. The estimate in Chapter 1 relies on the assumption that the running away rate amongst young people not included in the survey was equal to that for young people in the survey. Some justification for this assumption is provided by the link between truancy and running away presented in Chapter 2. This would suggest that, if anything, the incidence of running away amongst young people not in school when the survey was carried out would be higher than that for young people who were present. The estimates of the proportion of young people running from residential care in Chapter 5 are very rough, as noted in that chapter.

In-depth interviews with young people

Method of contacting young people

21 of the 28 young people interviewed were contacted through their use of Leeds Safe House - a refuge for young people who run away or are forced to leave where they live. The remainder were contacted through a variety of sources - mostly other professionals.

Characteristics of the sample

17 of the young people were female and 11 were male.
The age distribution was:
13 years old - 1 person
14 years old - 4 people
15 years old - 18 people
16 years old - 3 people
17 years old - 1 person
18 years old - 1 person
26 of the young people described their origin as 'White' or 'English'. The remaining two young people described their origins as 'Caribbean' and 'English/Asian' respectively.
At least 16 of the young people had lived in residential care.

Interview method

The interviews were semi-structured, covering a number of broad themes. Where possible, and with the young person's consent, the interview was tape recorded and transcribed word for word. In these cases (17 young people) the young person was shown the transcription and any alterations made, and the recording was then erased.

Ethics of interviewing

A policy was drawn up regarding the rights of young people involved in the research. The main points of this policy were:

- The young person should be given detailed information about the research and its uses so that they were in a position to make an informed choice about whether to participate
- The young person had the right to withdraw their consent at any time - including the right to withdraw information previously given.
- The information would be stored anonymously and confidentially and would only be accessible to workers directly involved in the research.
- The information would not be published in a way that could lead to the young person being identified.

An additional aspect of this policy was a statement of exceptions to the guarantee of confidentiality, which were fully explained to the young person before the interview began.

Copies of the policy are available from the address at the end of this appendix.

Interviews with professionals

The interviews with professionals in contact with young people were carried out in the development stage of the research. A range of professionals were approached in three areas of Leeds with differing demographic characteristics. Interviews were carried out face-to-face and notes were recorded in a standard format. The interviews provided information which was valuable in the development of the research plan. They also produced a number of key findings which have been discussed in the main body of the report.

Further information on the research methodology can be obtained from: Gwyther Rees, Leeds Safe House, c/o The Children's Society, Prudential House, 28-40 Blossom Street, York YO2 2AQ.

REFERENCES

Abrahams, C. and Mungall, R. (1992) *Runaways: Exploding the myths*. NCH.

Brennan, T., Huizinga, D. and Elliott, D. (1978) *The Social Psychology of Runaways*. Lexington Books.

1991 Census, County Report: West Yorkshire (Part 1) (1992) HMSO.

Children in Care in England (1993) Department of Health.

Ek, C. and Steelman, L. (1988) "Becoming a runaway - from the accounts of youthful runners" in *Youth and Society*, Vol.19, no.3, March 1988.

Fletcher, B. (1993) *Not just a name - the views of young people in foster and residential care*. National Consumer Council.

Frost, N. and Stein, M. (1989) *The Politics of Child Welfare*. Harvester Wheatsheaf.

Hier, S., Korboot, P. and Schweitzer, R. (1990) "Social adjustment and symptomatology in two types of homeless adolescents: runaways and throwaways" in *Adolescence*, Vol. XXV, no.100, Winter 1990.

Newman, C. (1988) *Young runaways - findings from Britain's first safe house*. The Children's Society.

Simons, R. and Whitbeck, L. (1991) "Running away during adolescence as a precursor to adult homelessness" in *Social Service Review*, June 1991.

Warner, N., Clough, D., Gozzard, A., Hughes, J., Iles, F., Jones, A., Lansdown, R., Proctor, D., Thomas, S., and White, R. [The Committee of Inquiry into the Selection, Development and Management of Staff in Children's Homes] (1992) *Choosing with Care*. Department of Health. HMSO.

The Children's Society

The Children's Society is a national voluntary organization of the Church of England and the Church in Wales. It exists to work for children and young people, irrespective of their race or religious belief.

The Children's Society runs 126 projects throughout England and Wales, including:

- working with young people living on the street.
- providing independent living units for young people leaving care.
- promoting the rights of children and young people.
- family centres and neighbourhood groups in local communities where families are under stress, often feeling isolated and powerless to improve their lives.
- working with young offenders, offering them a constructive alternative to crime.
- residential and day care for children and young people with disabilities.
- helping children and young people with special needs to find new families.
- offering independent guardians ad litem for children involved in care proceedings.

The Children's Society is committed to raising public awareness of issues affecting children and young people and to promoting their welfare and rights in matters of public policy. The Society produces a wide range of publications, including reports, briefing papers and educational material.

For further information about the work of The Children's Society or to obtain a full publications list, please contact:

> The Publications Department
> The Children's Society
> Edward Rudolf House
> Margery Street
> London WC1X 0JL
> tel. 071-837 4299.

Printed by The Grange Press, Southwick, West Sussex